AF326561

A Family's Civil War Struggles

Stories of My Ancestors of Shelton Laurel, North Carolina

By

Maynard Scott Shelton

A Family's Civil War Struggles

Stories of My Ancestors of Shelton Laurel, North Carolina

By

Maynard Scott Shelton

Published in the United States of America

by

The Tennessee Publishing House
Belle Arden Run Estate,
496 Mountain View Drive
Mosheim, TN 37818-3524
First Edition, Copyright October 2014

Permissions

All material has been received and authenticated by the author and placed with permission wherever it has been obtainable.

Any Scripture has been taken from the King James Version of the *Holy Bible* (KJV).

All pictures, unless otherwise noted and given permission for their usage, have been taken from the free Internet pictures distributed throughout various image and photo sites.

Disclaimer

This document is an original work of the author. It may include reference to information commonly known or freely available to the general public. Any resemblance to other published information is purely coincidental. The author has in no way attempted to use material not of his own origination. Any material that has been used which has been submitted to the author anonymously without representation is regretted if used without authentication of its origin. The Tennessee Publishing House disclaims any association with or responsibility for the ideas, opinions or facts as expressed by the author of this book. No dialog is totally accurate or precise.

Printed in the United States of American
Library of Congress
Cataloging-in-Publication
ISBN: 978-1-58275-295-2

Cover Design: Maynard Scott Shelton and Kellie Warren

Dedication

I dedicate this work to the memory of my late father, Edd, my late mother Velma, all of my deceased uncles and aunts, my grandfathers and grandmothers, and their parents, grandparents, great-grandparents, and great-great grandparents. Also, I want to dedicate these writings to my currently living uncles and aunts; Zelois, Zettie, Dot, Doris, Louise, Odell and Verna Lee, Barnabas and Frances, Hazel, Crate, Arlin and Margaret, Clifford and Mary, and Gerald and Nancy. (Also Beulah, Ann, Sharon, and Brenda). Since I have no children of my own to perpetuate the Shelton name, this manuscript is my way of passing the name to future generations.

I challenge the reader of this manuscript to question the truthfulness of the contents by doing his or her own research. "If information is always accepted as truth, then knowledge will never grow." (Quote of the author)

Maynard Scott Shelton

Acknowledgements

I would like to thank two teaching colleagues of mine for their input in helping me with phrasing and punctuation with this work. Mrs. Carla Kesterson and Mrs. Linda Humphreys were most helpful with their critical reviews, and advice. Mrs. Humphreys was surprised (as was I) to find from reading this manuscript that she and I are slightly related from the Haire branch of our ancestral genealogy. Also earning words of thanks are Mrs. Jean Ottinger and Miss Shelby Standridge for providing technical advice and assistance in scanning and inserting photographs and government documents.

I would also like to thank my field-test subjects, Dale, Darla, and Teresa Shelton, and Allen Atkinson for reading this work and providing valuable feedback.

Lastly, I would like to thank my aunt Zelois Shelton Hensley for developing and nurturing my intense interest in the history of my wonderful family.

Maynard Scott Shelton

Foreword

Maynard Scott Shelton captures the history of the small community of Shelton Laurel in western North Carolina. The independent nature of the brave pioneers who founded Shelton Laurel, as well as their freedom-loving descendants who fought to preserve democracy, is well documented by the research conducted by Mr. Shelton. The folks who lived and died in Shelton Laurel represent what Frederick Law Olmsted called, "rugged individualism" preferring the outside world to leave them alone allowing the residents to live their lives in peace and harmony in their beautiful mountain community.

Mr. Shelton personalizes the lives of his relatives with stories that capture the reader's imagination. He gives us fascinating insight into his relatives' life struggles and how their independent nature influenced the lives of each succeeding generation. Mr. Shelton shares with the reader not only his devotion for his relatives, but also imparts his love for the beautiful, peaceful, and mountainous region of the community of Shelton Laurel.

Maynard Shelton and I have worked together for thirteen years at South Greene High School and he is by far the absolutely best chemistry and physics teacher I have ever known. The evidence is in the number of students whom he has positively influenced and who are contributing to our society. We share a love of history and I was elated when asked to write the *Foreword* for his book, *A Family's Civil War Struggles*.

It has been an honor and a privilege to not only work with him but to know him on a personal level. I would recommend everyone not only enjoy Mr. Shelton's book, but also to travel to Shelton Laurel, North Carolina and to enjoy the beauty of this wondrous place.

Cindy Bowman, Ed.D.
Principal, South Greene High School
Greene County, Tennessee

Table of Contents

Chapter One
European and Colonial Sheltons

My name is Maynard Scott Shelton, and ever since I can remember, I've heard about and read books about the magnificent history and heritage of the Shelton name. Also, ever since I can remember, I have thought that the absolute most beautiful place on the planet was Shelton Laurel, North Carolina, especially the upper Mill Creek section. My great-grandparents settled in this section around one hundred and thirty years ago, and I'm proud to say that I own a small portion of the original homestead. The creek is named "Mill Creek" because my great-grandfather ran a grist mill and ground corn into meal for the people of the community. Ever since I was a small child I was aware of a couple of assumptions and sayings about the place. "Shelton Laurel is a part of 'Bloody Madison'." Also, "Shelton Laurel is a rough country; strangers aren't welcome and don't linger." As a Shelton, I really couldn't understand how anyone could form a negative opinion about the place and the people. My father, Edd Shelton, always said, *"Sheltons are the finest people in the world if you give them everything they want and never ask them for anything."* I suppose this could be said of any family name, but I think what he was implying was that Sheltons wanted more than anything else to simply be left alone. This manuscript is my attempt to tie together the people and the place. Most of this writing will focus on events occurring during the War Between the States, as I think this time period, with the events and atrocities, is the origin of attitudes like "Bloody Madison" and the roughness of Shelton Laurel and its inhabitants. I would prefer our history books call the conflict "War Between the States" instead of "Civil War", as I have never been able to find anything "civil" about war. To me, "Civil War" is an oxymoron, and I'll let the English scholars explain that word for those who do not know.

It is certainly not going to be the intent of this author to get into genealogy, as numerous books have been written and published on Shelton genealogy. The wheel doesn't need to be re-invented. I will, however, refer to genealogy on occasion just to tie my own ancestral lineage to a particular story. The original people living in the area later to become known as Shelton Laurel were Native Americans. When I was a child my uncle Fred showed me a collection of artifacts that he had found over the years while working in tobacco and tomato fields. Also, later in life a friend and I were hiking a portion of the Appalachian Trail near the headwaters of Shelton Laurel Creek when we discovered a beautiful arrowhead, shaped in the Mississipian style that predated the Cherokees by a thousand years. The first white settlers didn't come to the area until after the Revolutionary War when the Native Americans were defeated and driven from the area.

Genealogy books have traced the European Shelton lineage back to the Druids of England in 1300 B.C., the Caesars of Rome in 100 B.C., and Mohammed the Prophet in 600 A.D. All of these are descendants of Ishmael, who was the brother of Isaac and son of Abraham *Genesis 18:15,* and *21:3.* Other notable historical names that the Sheltons are direct descendants of include Constantine, Charles Martel, and Charlemagne. To read some of the genealogies that have been published, you would think that Adam and Eve were Sheltons! According to Mildred Campbell Whitaker, author of *The Sheltons of England and America,* the Sheltons are direct descendants of fourteen of the twenty-five barons who forced King John to sign the *Magna Carta* in 1215. One of the most confusing impediments to figuring out the genealogy of the Sheltons is the various ways the name is spelled. Whitaker points out in her book, *"It seems that one of the evidences of culture in the early days was the number of ways a man could spell his name. Four different spellings; Chilton, Skelton, Shelton, and Sheldon, have been recorded on the birth, marriage, and death notice of the same individual!"* Other variations of the Shelton name include Chelton, Carleton, Charleton, and Shilton. Whitaker insists that all these are variations of the same name, Shelton. Another obstacle in deciphering Shelton genealogy is the duplication of first names. There are twelve generations of Sheltons from 1200 A.D. until 1500 A.D., and every one of them were either "John" or

"Ralph". Even today Sheltons like to name their male children after fathers or grandfathers.

Shelton families were living in Norfolk and Suffolk counties of England as early as 792 A.D. John de Shelton, 1st Lord of Shelton, combined his manor at Stradbrooke, Suffolk to the "Priory of Butley" in Norfolk. Most of the male descendants of the 1st Lord of Shelton had the title of "Sir" in their name, indicating knighthood. Knighthood was not inherited, however, it was earned, mostly for valor in battle. Sir John Shelton, 21st Lord of Shelton, married Lady Anne Boleyn, aunt of Queen Anne Boleyn. Sir John was High Sheriff of Norfolk in 1504, and was knighted in 1509. When Princess Elizabeth was persecuted during her sister's (Queen Mary) reign, she fled to Norfolk and hid out at Sir John and Lady Shelton's mansion. Later, when Elizabeth was crowned Queen, she summoned Sir John's family to the Palace where his descendants lived during the remainder of her reign. Sir John and Lady Shelton's great-grandson was Sir Ralph Shelton, 26th Lord of Shelton. He was born in 1560, and was knighted in 1607 at Theobald. Sir Ralph sold the Norfolk estates in 1606. He served England as Minister to Spain and Secretary to the Prince of Wales. Sir Ralph married Jane West, daughter of William West, also known as Lord Delaware. One of their sons, Thomas Shelton, invented the first process of shorthand in 1630. Another one of their sons, James Shelton, came to Virginia in 1610 with his uncle, Lord Delaware II, and was the first Shelton in America.

His father, Sir Ralph Shelton, remained in England and was later killed at the battle of Isle de Rhe on July 22, 1628.

James Shelton was a very influential man in Jamestown, Virginia. He was a member of the first courts of America in 1619, and in 1624, he was a member of the Council of the London Company of Virginia. The Sheltons had acquired their own ships and did a large amount of business with Bermuda. In 1630, James, his wife Anne, and their children moved to Barbados, Bermuda. The Governor of Bermuda, Captain Henry Woodhouse, was a kinsman of Sir Ralph Shelton, James' father. Two of James' sons, John and Ralph, were ship owners and merchants who made large sales of commodities to Virginia planters. By the time he died in 1668, James and his sons had acquired large tracts of lands in both Bermuda and Virginia. In checking with historians, the two most prominent "commodities" coming out of Bermuda in the 1600s were slaves and rum. I don't know how the Sheltons that lived in Bermuda came to be so wealthy, and I'm not going to research that, as I fear what I might find. The reader can feel free to do so.

In tracing my own genealogy, James' grandson Peter (son of Ralph of Bermuda) was born in 1664 in Bermuda, but by the 1680s was living in Middlesex County, VA. His wife was Susannah Jackson and they had three children, Ralph, Peter, Jr., and Susannah. Peter died in 1718. His son Ralph (1685-1733) married Mary Crispen and they had a large family. One of Ralph and Mary's sons was Ralph Shelton, born in 1709, in Middlesex County, Virginia. This Ralph married a woman named Mary Daniel. Ralph Shelton and Mary Daniel had several children, with one being named James, born in 1734, in Middlesex County. This James married a woman named Jencia (I haven't been able to confirm her maiden name) and served as a Captain in the Revolutionary War. James and Jencia's son, Roderick, took his wife, Sarah Ursula Briggs and their young family out of eastern Virginia and moved to the wild backwoods of what is now western North Carolina shortly after America gained her independence from England. Their son, David, is the author's great-great-great-great grandfather, and who Shelton Laurel, North Carolina is named after.

Another son of James Shelton (1610, Virginia) was Thomas Shelton. Thomas' descendants were the Sheltons who owned the large Virginia plantations of Currioman in Westmoreland County, Carotoman in Lancaster County, and Rural Plains in Hanover County. Captain John Shelton of Rural Plains had a daughter whose name was Sarah. Sarah married eighteen-year-old Patrick Henry when she was sixteen. They had six children, and Sarah died shortly thereafter. If it hadn't been for the support of his father-in-law John Shelton, Patrick Henry could have never finished college and become a statesman. He probably would have never had the opportunity to give the famous "Give me liberty or give me death!" speech. Captain John Shelton was killed in the Battle of Brandywine (September 11, 1777) in the Revolutionary War.

Other prominent names associated with the Shelton name include Martha (Patty) Wales. Her first husband was Bathurst Shelton. After his death, she married Thomas Jefferson, the third President of the United States. General John Ross Key married Ann Roche Shelton, and their son was none other than Francis Scott Key, author of the "Star Spangled Banner." Also, the Battle of the Wilderness in the Civil War was fought on property owned by two Shelton brothers. There are many other interesting items and facts concerning Sheltons of both England and America, but I would now like to focus the remainder of this writing on the Shelton family that settled in what is now called Shelton Laurel, North Carolina, and their way of life before, during, and after the War Between the States.

CATHERINE
MILLER
SEFTON
BORN ABOUT 1773

**The burial site of David and Catherine Miller Shelton
in the Judith Shelton Cemetery in Shelton Laurel,
North Carolina.**

Chapter Two
To Secede from the Union (Or Not)

No period of time in the history of the United States has ever been as tumultuous, dividing, heart wrenching, or bloody as the 1860s. Washington politicians were heatedly arguing whether or not the federal government had any right to impose upon individual states laws, opinions, or ideologies. Individual states argued that they alone should be able to decide whether or not to accept or allow certain practices. At the heart of this issue was the question of the right of one man to actually own or possess another. The practice of slavery had been around since biblical times, with the most notable *Bible* "character" being Joseph, who was sold into bondage of Egypt by his jealous brothers *Genesis 37:28.* But the founding fathers of our country had written into the *Declaration of Independence* that *"all men are created equal."* Was the Black man a man? Obviously so, but the states wanting the right to obtain and possess slaves obviously thought that some men must have been more "equal" than others.

The plantation and cotton-producing states of Alabama, Georgia, South Carolina, and Virginia led the way in "drawing the line" between states' rights and the meddling government bureaucracy. Western Tennessee and eastern North Carolina had large plantation owners who utilized slaves, so they were quick to get on the bandwagon of secession. However, the poorer small-time mountain farmers of western North Carolina and eastern Tennessee had nothing to do with slavery. Furthermore, many of their fathers and grandfathers had helped fight and win the Revolutionary War. The federal government loomed large in their eyes; they were not about to turn their back on it.

The 1860 census of Madison County reported 137 Sheltons living in 25 households, almost all within the Shelton Laurel, Big Laurel, and Little Laurel regions. All were brothers, sisters or cousins, and all were descendants of Roderick Shelton, Sr. (a Revolutionary War veteran) and his sons David, Martin, and Roderick, Jr. Earlier census records indicate that while most Sheltons had large families and were poor according to the plantation owners' standards, David did own two slaves, a man and his wife. They were evidently very well thought of and liked, possibly even considered a part of the family, because when they died, they were buried in the family cemetery alongside the plots that were reserved for David and his wife Catherine.

Other notable families that had moved into the Laurel region and were living there in 1860 included the Cutshalls, (Gotshalls), Hensleys, Tweeds, Franklins, Nortons, and Landers. The cities of Washington and

Raleigh probably seemed a long way removed for these families, and they thought that the political events of the time would never have any bearing or effect on them. Not that they were living in blissful harmony with each other, for Shelton Laurel had its internal strife long before the war began. In May 1854, an edition of the *Asheville Spectator* newspaper reported that three men, one by the name of James Shelton, had killed Drury Norton. Norton's wife was Nancy Shelton Norton, James' sister. (Nancy and James were children of Roderick Shelton, Jr., and Rachel Moore). Did Norton deserve killing? Had James Shelton taken the law into his own hands? After all, "law" was almost non-existent in the Laurel part of Madison County anyway. The answers to these questions have gotten clouded with the passage of time, but the incident clearly shows that there was personal turmoil between the people who lived in the Laurel region, and later James Shelton was acquitted, claiming that Drury Norton had pulled a knife on him, so the killing was self-defense (Nancy Shelton Norton and James Shelton are the topics of another chapter).

The mountaineers of Shelton Laurel seldom traveled to town, and when you consider that the nearest town was Marshall, the county seat of newly formed Madison County, one could understand why. The little township had a long street parallel to a river and a mountain. Even today when walking along Main Street, you get the feeling that the mountain ridge is trying its best to push the one street and two rows of houses and small businesses right into the French Broad River.

Two occurrences that would bring the mountain people to town were: court day, and Election Day. On May 13, 1861, such an occurrence was going on. The state legislature had each county in North Carolina hold a referendum on the question of seceding from the United States and joining other southern states in forming a Confederacy. The Piedmont and coastal regions of the state were overwhelmingly in favor of secession, but it was a different matter in the mountain counties. Divisions were cut and dried; the affluent people of the townships were strongly in favor of secession, the poor mountain farmers against secession.

The little town of Marshall was packed the day of the vote. It is often said that whiskey and differing opinions don't mix, and that was soon to be played out in the quaint, usually quiet town. Sheriff Ransom P. Merrill was walking up and down the street, greeting his friends and harassing his enemies. He was loudly expressing his opinion and doing quite a bit of drinking of some liquor that had no doubt been manufactured by some mountaineer alongside some cold mountain stream, with the aid of some fermented corn and sugar. The sheriff, being a town dweller and friends with the richest and most powerful men of the county, was strongly in favor of secession, and the drunker he got, the louder he got.

Finally no longer able to contain his excitement, the sheriff waved his hat, reared back his head, and shouted *"Huzzah for Jeff Davis and the Confederacy!!!"* From the crowd came an enthusiastic reply, *"Hurrah for Washington and the Union!!!"* The sheriff spun around, spotted the poor mountain farmer who had yelled the reply, drew his pistol, and began advancing toward the man. At that point the Lincolnite farmer hurriedly withdrew, while the crowd became silent. Shortly afterwards, the sheriff observed another man standing nearby with a pistol visible from the waistband of his trousers. The sheriff again drew his gun and yelled, *"What are you doing here with your gun?"* It became apparent to the crowd that Sheriff Merrill was just itching to shoot somebody before the morning was over. About that time the sheriff spied a man by the name of Nealey Tweed. Mr. Tweed was well known throughout the county as being a strong Union man. Mr. Wellman in his book *The Kingdom of Madison* reports that Mr. Tweed was a Clerk of the Superior Court and a former friend of the sheriff. Nealey Tweed was a Justice of the Peace for Yancey County in the 1840s (Shelton Laurel was a part of Yancey County from 1833 to 1851 when Madison County was formed). More recently, however, the sheriff and Mr. Tweed had exchanged heated words on several occasions.

When Sheriff Merrill saw Nealey Tweed in the crowd, he raised his pistol and fired. Mr. Tweed reacted by lunging to one side. The bullet missed Tweed, but hit his son

Elisha who was standing behind him. The bullet went clean through the boy's arm and lodged in his ribcage. The sheriff suddenly realized that he was surrounded by far more enemies than his pistol had shots, so he ran to a nearby house, bolted up the stairs to a second story window facing the street and from the window yelled, *"Come up here, all you damned Black Republicans, and take a shot about with me!!"* Nealey Tweed responded by shooting and wounding the sheriff from the street. About that time the constable showed up, gained entrance to the house, and went upstairs to take the bleeding sheriff into custody.

However, Mr. Tweed was right behind the constable on the stairs, and as soon as the bedroom door flung open, Nealey Tweed shot and killed the sheriff at close range with a double-barrel shotgun. At that point, pandemonium broke loose in the street, with Unionists and Secessionists arguing and swinging at each other. During all this, Nealey Tweed and his wounded son escaped, started on their journey to Kentucky that night, and joined the Union Army's 4th Tennessee Infantry.

Nealey Tweed took a fever and eventually died about a year later, and his son survived the war. Mr. Tweed was married to my great-great-great aunt Lucinda Hensley. She was an older sister of two of my great-great grandfathers, John and Bill Hensley. They were the children of Charles Hensley and Rhoda Franklin. Bill Hensley's story is the focus of another chapter. By the way, the results of the May 13th election were 28 votes for Secessionist delegates and 144 votes for the Unionist delegates.

I've wondered if that included Sheriff Merrill's vote. North Carolina seceded from the Union on May 20, 1861. Two of Sheriff Merrill's closest friends in Marshall were Dr. James Keith and Lawrence Allen. This incident was the start of turmoil between these men and the people of Shelton Laurel which would eventually culminate in the role that these two future colonels of the 64th Confederate Regiment would play in the Shelton Laurel Massacre.

After the original Sheltons of western North Carolina began their families and homesteads in the late 1700s and early 1800s, the population of Sheltons began to grow quite rapidly. Other family names such as Hensley, Cutshall, Norton, Franklin, and Haire had migrated into the area, and the Sheltons married into these families, as well as marrying their Shelton cousins. They fulfilled the word of the Lord when He commanded *to ". . . multiply and replenish the earth ..." Genesis 1:28 (KJV)* by having large families, and most of the babies born to Shelton families were boys, for some reason. Life in Shelton Laurel, Big Laurel, and Little Laurel was overall pretty good. It was a hard life in that you had to work hard hunting and raising crops for food, felling trees to build your cabin, and cutting wood for fire and kindling, but you were pretty much your own boss.

That lifestyle led to a whole generation of mountain people that were extremely independent. Some got schooled in reading and writing, but most were illiterate. Some got religion for the right purposes, while others used the concept of religion for their own good. Once a travelling preacher observed a mountaineer with a rifle hiding in the laurels beside the main trail, and he yelled to the man,

"Hey, what are you doing hiding up there in the thicket?" The pious mountaineer replied, *"Ride on by stranger, I'm ah waitin' fer Jim Johnson, and with the help of the Laud, I'm ah gonna blow his damn head off!"* The birth of Christ was observed on January 6th, in keeping with the old European tradition. It certainly was more of an observance than a celebration, as the tradition of gift-giving wasn't practiced much. The mountaineer families taught their children that the ultimate gift to a sinful world was God's gift of His son, Jesus. Read: *John 3:16.* Christmas being recognized as December 25th didn't officially begin in America until President Grant's tenure in the early 1870s.

As the patriarchs of the families started dying, large tracts of lands were divided into smaller tracts for the surviving children, with the youngest child usually receiving the home (normally a one or two-room cabin). The mountain people had little reason to go to town. They were very self-sustaining in that they provided their own food, made their own clothes, whittled and shaped their own tools, and used herbal medicines to treat their illnesses. The one staple that they could not produce on their own was salt. They didn't use salt in the same way that we use it today. They didn't need salt to flavor their food, but to preserve their meat.

Before the days of electricity and deep freezers, people used cold, trickling streams from springs to refrigerate their perishable food, and the mountaineers built a little shed over their best spring, called a springhouse. They kept their butter and milk in containers submerged in the cold spring water. However, to preserve their meat so it would last sufficiently, they had to salt it down. Salt was especially needed during the hog killing season of November and December.

During the decades leading up to the Civil War, growers of livestock and poultry would drive their animals hundreds of miles to markets, much the same way that the cowboys of the West would drive large herds of cattle to northern markets a few decades later. The route that the drivers of mainly hogs and turkeys would take from Tennessee, Kentucky, western Virginia, and even as far away as Ohio came through western North Carolina by way of a road called the Buncombe Turnpike. This road for the most part followed the edge of the French Broad River from present-day Newport, Tennessee and upstream to Warm Springs, North Carolina, then to Lapland (Marshall), and on to Asheville, then to the mountain gaps that led to the Piedmont, and finally to Columbia and Charleston, South Carolina.

Stock stands with taverns began to spring up along the route to give the drivers a place to pen their herds or roost their birds for the night. Eventually, there were fifteen such stands along the forty-seven mile stretch of the road from the TN-NC state line at Paint Rock to Asheville. The farmers of the Laurel region didn't raise herds of hogs or flocks of turkeys that needed to be driven to South Carolina, but they were able to profit by selling bushels of corn and chestnuts (the American Chestnut tree was the dominant hardwood tree of the Southern Appalachian forests at that time) to the owners of the stock stands. The owners would in turn charge the drivers for the feeding of their herds or flocks. The stands were also stores where the drivers could purchase provisions for their trip. They usually didn't pay the stand owners immediately, but would pay them on their way back from South Carolina after they had sold their hogs or turkeys.

I apologize to the reader for the temporary divergence from the story. Now back to the need for salt. During the months of November and December of 1862, the salt mines of Saltville, Virginia were completely controlled by the Confederates, and salt became scarce in the little towns and communities. The merchants of Marshall, North Carolina who controlled the sale of salt were instructed by the Confederate authorities not to sell any salt to the mountain people of the Laurels and other mountain regions because of their loyalty to the Union. (The mountain people couldn't afford it, anyway. A sack of salt was priced at $100.)

When patrols of the 64th Confederate regiment were sent into the Laurel region to draft men for the army, they were met by stiff resistance, usually in the form of snipers or bushwhackers whom they far outnumbered but could never defeat because of the "gorilla-warfare" tactics used by the mountaineers. The Rebels would torture the mountain women and children, trying to get them to divulge the location of their men, but usually to no avail. When the need for salt came with the hog killing season of the fall of 1862, withholding the salt was a great way (they thought) to punish the Unionists of the mountains. Also, there had been bad blood between the citizens of the Laurel region and the main leaders of the 64th Rebel regiment ever since the vote of secession in May 1861. So when the mountaineers went to Marshall to purchase salt, they were rejected.

In early January, 1863, a group of about fifty men from the mountains invaded and raided the town of Marshall. Most of these men were reported to have been deserters from the 64th that had been conscripted into the Rebel army against their will. Their main objective was the salt stores, but some of them also pillaged some homes and stole clothes, blankets and other items. One of the homes that was broken into belonged to Col. Lawrence M. Allen, main commander of the 64th Confederate regiment. The regiment was called "Allen's Rangers" before it was given the 64th designation. Col. Allen's wife's kinsman Capt. John Peek was at Col. Allen's home that night and was wounded in the raid. He had originally been with the 16th Confederate regiment but when they marched away to the "big" war, he somehow got transferred back home to the 64th.

Two of Col. Allen's children were sick with scarlet fever, and the plunderers even stole the sick children's blankets. The men then took the salt and other things they had stolen and disappeared back into the mountains.

At the time of the Marshall raid, the 64th was in Bristol, Tennessee, near Saltville, Virginia guarding salt supplies there. When news of the raid reached them, acting Commander Col. James Keith met with Gen. Henry Heth (commander of all Rebel forces in East Tennessee at the time) and requested permission to take some companies of the 64th to Shelton Laurel to capture and punish those involved in the Marshall raid. He had no proof that anybody from Shelton Laurel had actually participated, but he saw it as an excellent opportunity to get back at the people and the region that had been a thorn in his side since 1861. Gen. Heth informed Keith that he didn't want to be troubled with prisoners. Keith recognized that statement as an underlying assumption to mean that he could do as he pleased with anyone who was captured.

By January 15, 1863, two columns of Rebel soldiers were converging on Shelton Laurel. One column, led by Col. Keith, came in from the crest or the head of Shelton Laurel, while the other column, led by Col. Allen, who entered Shelton Laurel from the White Rock area. The weather was bitterly cold, and blizzard-like conditions prevailed. As the soldiers came to homesteads and cabins they tortured women and children in the most barbaric manner to try to find out where the men were. Two women were hanged until nearly dead, and another woman was tied to a tree just out of reach of her crying infant who had been lain on the cold ground, and several women were beaten almost to the point of death.

The two Rebel columns finally met each other in the area of Bill Shelton's farm (the author's great-great-great grandfather). Then a skirmish ensued with some of the Laurel citizens at that time. After the "roundup", the Rebels had captured fifteen people, mostly older men and boys. These poor captives had been taken peacefully at their homes, offering no resistance except maybe running out the back door to avoid capture. Of the fifteen, at most five might have been involved in the Marshall raid. As they declared their innocence, Col. Allen told them that they would be taken to Knoxville to stand trial. They were confined in the Judith Shelton house over the weekend. Late on the first night a rider from Marshall arrived with bad news for Col. Allen. His six-year-old son had died of scarlet fever, and his four-year-old daughter wasn't expected to survive the night. Col. Allen left at daybreak the next morning by horseback and arrived in Marshall about 10:00 A. M., but his daughter was already dead. He and his wife buried the children, and by the next day he was back in Shelton Laurel with his soldiers.

On the night of January 18, 1863, one of the captives named Pete McCoy escaped. Family tradition states that Pete was a Mason, and so was the Rebel soldier guarding the cabin that night. Evidently the brotherhood of Masonry was stronger than the need to perform guard duty, and the guard allowed Pete to escape. On Monday morning, January 19, 1863, the captured were marched out of the cabin to the road. Twelve-year old Johnnie Norton had crawled under one of the beds and was sleeping, and the Rebels didn't notice him, so he was left in the cabin. Years later, Johnnie Norton became a preacher, and I'm sure he gave God the glory for sparing his life.

The accounts of the following portion of the story are mostly drawn from the book *Thrilling Adventures of Daniel Ellis*. Mr. Ellis published his autobiography in 1867, and he informs the reader that his informant was an eye witness to the horrific event that was about to transpire. Also, the newspaper article that was published in the July 24, 1863, edition of the *New York Times* was very informative.

The soldiers began marching their captives down the road, supposedly on their way to Knoxville. After about three miles, the captives were suddenly ordered to halt. (This occurred just down from the present-day Lance Wallin homestead, in the field at the end of the Jimmy Joe Shelton air strip and hanger). Five of the prisoners were ordered to form a line and kneel down. One of the older men by the name of David Shelton exclaimed, *"I would kneel to my God, but I shall not kneel to devils!"* Another prisoner, sixty-year old Joe Woods suddenly realized what was happening and cried out, *"For God's sake men, are you not going to shoot us? If you're going to murder us, at least give us time to pray!"*

Another prisoner reminded Col. Keith of the promise of a trial, but was told Col. Allen, who made the promise, was not in charge, that Keith was in charge. (This was true. Col. Allen had been suspended from command for six months because of drunkenness while on duty, but he remained with his troops.) Keith gave the order to fire, but the soldiers hesitated. Keith yelled, *"If you don't fire when the order is given, you will take the prisoners' place!"* Again the order to fire was given. Four of the five captives fell dead. The fifth was wounded in the abdomen, but was soon relieved of his pain by a second volley of fire.

The next five prisoners were ordered to line up and kneel. Among them was thirteen-year-old David Shelton. He pleaded, *"Please don't shoot me in my forehead, for I do not wish my blood to spoil these little curls, which my mother loves so dearly!"* The command to fire was again given, and again four captives fell dead. The fifth wounded captive was young David Shelton. He crawled toward an officer and pleaded, *"You have killed my old father and my brother; you have shot me in both arms. I forgive you all this, I can get well. Let me go home to my mother and sisters."* They dragged the boy back to the execution spot and shot him dead. Then the remaining three prisoners took their turn and were shot dead. The soldiers then dug a shallow trench and threw the bodies in it. Occasionally one of the bodies would involuntarily twitch, and the soldiers would begin beating the body with their rifle butts. One of the soldiers had a hoe, and he would start chopping on bodies that he thought had moved. One of the soldiers remarked, *"I never saw men so hard to kill."* When the burying job was almost finished, a Rebel soldier named Sgt. N. B. D. Jay, a Virginian assigned to the 64th, jumped on the pile of bodies and yelled, *"Pat Juba for me boys, while I dance the damned scoundrels down to and through Hell!"* Now that Shelton Laurel had been punished, most all of the soldiers moved on. Watching all this from the laurel thickets was a completely shocked and astonished Pete McCoy, the prisoner who had previously escaped. One of the murdered men was his brother-in-law, and two of the victims were his nephews.

Family members of the victims, mainly women, requested the detail of soldiers that remained for permission to move the bodies and give them a proper burial. They were given permission, but were told that if they shed a tear, they would be shot on the spot. When they arrived at the site of the massacre to retrieve the bodies, they discovered that hogs had rooted up one of the slain and had partially eaten the poor victim's head. The bodies were moved and buried in a common grave in what is now known as the Judith Shelton Cemetery. The victims' names and ages are as follows:

James Shelton, Sr., age 36

James Shelton, Jr., age 16

David Shelton, age 13

William R. Shelton, age 21

Azariah Shelton, age 16

David Shelton, age 56

Rod Shelton (Stob Rod), age 48

Hallen Moore, age 25

Wade Moore, age 20

Joe Woods, age 60

James Metcalfe, age 40

Ellison King, age 24

Jasper Chandler, age 15

News of the massacre spread, and by February, State Attorney A.S. Merrimon sent a letter to Governor Zebulon Vance describing the atrocity. Governor Vance was outraged, and demanded the resignation of James Keith from the army. He also demanded that Keith face criminal murder charges. By May 1863, Keith was forced to resign his commission, and was wanted by the state of North Carolina for murder. He had been allowed to ride out of Knoxville a free man, so he remained at large. He was finally captured in the spring of 1865 and placed in prison. Eventually, he was transferred to the Marshall jail to await trial, which finally began in December of 1868. He was to be tried thirteen different times for thirteen different murders. On February 21, 1869, he escaped from the Buncombe County jail and was never heard from again. Many years later, his Marshall property was sold through a landholding company, and it is thought that he ended up in Arkansas.

Col. Allen was never implicated in the murders, as he was not in command at the time. His trouble with the Confederate authority continued, however, and he was forced to resign his commission in the spring of 1864. Afterwards he moved to Arkansas, later to Colorado, and finally to Arizona. Gen. Henry Heth was never implicated in the massacre, even though he was the commanding general who "didn't want to be troubled with prisoners." Shortly after his meeting with Col. Keith, he was transferred to the Army of Northern Virginia to serve the remainder of the war with his old friend, Robert E. Lee. His bravery and leadership in the Battle of Chancellorsville earned him a promotion to Major General.

Meanwhile, the people of Shelton Laurel weren't punished by the massacre, they were empowered by it. More and more men joined the Union army, enough for an entire regiment. The 2nd and 3rd North Carolina

Mounted Volunteers were formed, and the Confederates had an even harder time operating in the mountains. Shelton Laurel became a Union stronghold, and home militia were brave enough to drill out in the open. Shortly after the massacre, Pete McCoy traveled to Flag Pond, Tennessee to the home of a gunsmith Ambrose Lawing, to have a rifle made. He told Mr. Lawing that he wanted a .44 caliber long rifle, one to hunt men, not game. Mr. Lawing produced the rifle but wouldn't charge McCoy any money for it. He obviously was a strong Union man. Over the course of the next three years, family tradition states that Pete McCoy killed between twenty and thirty Rebel soldiers of the 64th that were involved in the Shelton Laurel Massacre with that rifle by using sniper and bushwhacking tactics. Each time a Rebel soldier fell dead from his gun, McCoy would pat the stock of the rifle and murmur, "Sweet revenge." The widows of some of the victims applied for a Federal government pension in 1869. The United States Senate approved the pension payments, but the bill got bogged down in the Congress. It was re-submitted in January of 1874, and was then sent to the Committee on Pensions. There was no proof or evidence that any of the victims had ever been in the Union Army. On January 22, 1874, the bill was tabled indefinitely and was never considered again.

One has to wonder, with major battles of the Civil War resulting in thousands of casualties on both sides in a single day, what is the significance of thirteen deaths in an obscure place like Shelton Laurel? The answer is the difference between the "past" and "history." History is studied by scholars searching for the big picture, whereas the past is passed down from generation to generation within families. In learning the "past" you find out how "history" affected your great-great-great grandparents.

In her book, *The French Broad*, Wilma Dykeman sums up the atrocity in Shelton Laurel by stating, *"Much has been written of the large battles and decisive deaths of the War Between the States, but nowhere is there a microcosm more chill (sic) and revealing than this episode of war at its heart and core."*

In A. S. Merrimon's letter to Governor Vance, he listed the name "Joseph Cleandon, age 15" as a victim, and he did not include the name "Jasper Chandler." Family records and the gravesite monument doesn't include the name "Joseph Cleandon." It is this author's opinion that Merrimon's list was incorrect, as I trust the family records. If, however, Joseph Cleandon and Jasper Chandler were both slain, that would make fourteen victims and not thirteen.

There is a historical marker at the junction of NC highways 208 and 212, where Little Laurel Creek and Shelton Laurel Creek merge that depicts the Shelton Laurel Massacre. This marker is eight miles from the actual site of the massacre, however. The only structure left of the Judith Shelton house where the victims were held captive is a sturdy rock chimney. The cemetery where the victims are buried is totally grown up with trees now, and a modern log house has been built at the edge of the cemetery. The only official marker in the cemetery is a marble monument containing the names of the victims that was placed on the common grave of the victims by two grandsons of James Shelton, Sr., in 1965. A stranger or visitor to the area would never know the location, but the descendants of the victims know, especially the ones who still live in Shelton Laurel.

Historical marker depicting the Shelton Laurel Massacre at the junction of NC 208 and NC 212 highways

Actual site of Shelton Laurel Massacre

Only remaining structure of the cabin where the massacre victims were held captive

Burial site of the Shelton Laurel Massacre victims in the Judith Shelton Cemetery

Chapter Four
The Heroine of the Laurels

Probably the best known woman who lived in the Laurel region in the 1800s was a lady by the name of Nancy Shelton Norton. Nancy's father and mother were Roderick Shelton, Jr. and Rachel Moore. Nancy was Bill Shelton's (the author's great-great-great grandfather) first cousin. Nancy was born in 1820 (some sources report 1825). Other children of Roderick, Jr. and Rachel were James (1822), George (1824), three daughters born between 1826 and 1830, Baxter (1832), Joseph (1834), Mary (1836), Lewis (1838), Roderick (1840), and Lurana (1844). George, Baxter, James, Roderick, and Lewis all served in the Union Army during the Civil War. Nancy married Drury Norton in 1841 and they had the following children: Catherine, Robert (Bayliss), James, George, Josiah, and Delaney Jane. Nancy and Drury built a cabin and lived in the area of the Laurel that is now called Guntertown (closer to Big Laurel Creek than Shelton Laurel Creek).

Drury and his brother-in-law James Shelton had conflicts, and in May 1854 James and two other men dragged Drury out of his cabin and beat him to death. All three were later acquitted by pleading self-defense. Nancy and her children maintained a close and loving relationship with James even though he helped kill their husband and father. In 1857, Nancy married George W. Franklin, Jr.

Many articles and even books have been written telling Nancy and her sons' story. One of the first authors to write about the story was Manley Wade Wellman in his book, *The Kingdom of Madison*. Wellman admits that the main source of his information was Bascom Lamar Lunsford, a Madison County folklorist of the early 1900s. Wellman's account has Nancy and her family as Rebel sympathizers and the soldiers who attacked her cabin Union, which is totally false. Because Wellman was a respected and well-known local author, other authors have used him as a reference to perpetuate the falseness of his account. (Trotter, *Bushwhackers, The Civil War in North Carolina, The Mountains*, and Paludan, *Victims, a True Story of the Civil War*). Had these authors done thorough and proper research, they would have refuted Wellman's account, and THIS author wouldn't feel compelled to write what REALLY happened. Another author's account of the story is a very truthful account. Larry LeMasters' article *"Die Like A Damned Dog"* is an excellently written, truthful account of Nancy's story. LeMasters' article was published in the August 1999 issue of *Civil War Times, Illustrated,* and I will attempt to paraphrase his account and add some family information as well.

After Nancy married Mr. Franklin, the Civil War came to the mountains in a harsh way. Almost all of the mountain people of the three Laurels (Shelton Laurel, Big Laurel, and Little Laurel) had Unionist sympathies but mainly wanted to be left alone. Shelton Laurel became a hideout for both Union and Confederate thugs and bushwhackers, and snipers from both sides utilized the rocks, boulders and laurel thickets very effectively. When organized troops came into the region, they were either the Confederate 64th or the Union 2nd. I have found no details indicating that these two groups actually lined up and fought a battle with each other. After the fall of Cumberland Gap in early September 1863, remnants of the 64th that weren't killed or captured began making their way back to Madison County. One of these groups came to the Laurel region to see what they could steal or plunder and on September 17, 1863, killed two Unionists, Tillman Landers and Robert Haire. (Robert Haire is the author's great-great-great grandfather. Robert Haire's great-grandfather is John Sevier, the first governor of Tennessee.)

The next day, on September 18, 1863, they came across the Norton cabin. At least two of Nancy's sons were reported to have joined the Union Army, so the Rebel detachment decided to see what trouble they could stir up. Seeing the Rebels dismounting, Nancy yelled to her husband and three sons who were at home (George was not home, which saved his life) *"Grab your guns and run those Rebels off!!"* Her husband Mr. Franklin was the first casualty, as he was shot in the leg at the springhouse (I'm assuming he lay motionless, pretending to be dead from that point on). Robert, James, and Josiah started returning fire from the cabin, hitting a couple of the Rebel soldiers (LeMasters' account has James Keith with the Rebels, but Keith had already been forced to resign his command, and was a fugitive hiding from the State of North Carolina because of his role in the murder of prisoners in January 1863, so I doubt if Keith was present at the Norton cabin). James ran out the door of the cabin and shot a Rebel officer off his horse. The Rebels returned fire and mortally wounded James as he ran for the cover of the split-rail fence. Robert then stepped out the door, possibly thinking he could help his wounded brother, and was killed instantly in a volley of gunfire.

About that time Josiah, who was only fifteen-years old, dove out a side window and crawled into the crawlspace under the cabin and started firing, wounding and killing several Rebels before they realized where the shots were coming from. One of the soldiers finally crawled under the cabin to shoot Josiah but was hit by gunfire and killed first. Another Rebel attempted to retrieve his fellow soldier's body, and Josiah promptly shot the second soldier in the head, killing him instantly. At this point in the battle the Rebels had suffered more casualties than the Nortons.

The remaining Rebel soldiers regrouped to discuss what could be done about the situation, and one of them suggested burning young Josiah out. That was agreed upon and some of them sneaked close enough to toss some burning sticks into the windows and onto the porch. Within minutes the cabin was blazing. Overcome with heat and smoke, Josiah had no choice but to crawl out from under the house. Nancy was being held by a couple of soldiers in the yard of the house. Before she was restrained, one of the soldiers had taken a shot at her at close range but had missed. His shot did, however, knock a lock of her hair off that was hanging outside her bonnet. At this point, Nancy was in a state of shock. She had just witnessed two of her sons being shot to death, and as Josiah crawled out from under the cabin, a Rebel soldier smashed Josiah's skull with the butt of a rifle. The attackers then collected their wounded and rode off, leaving their dead where they fell. After they were gone, a man named George Gahagan, along with the help of two black men, wrapped her sons' bodies in sheets and buried them in a common grave in what is now known as the Franklin Cemetery in Guntertown.

Concerning the whole terrible ordeal, Nancy was quoted as saying, *"You need not tell me self doesn't go a long way. As I came out of the burning house, one of the Confederate soldiers yelled 'Yonder is Nancy, the one we want!' I pulled my bonnet down over my eyes and didn't shed a tear. People standing around told the soldiers I was Mary Franklin, but when they left, I was like a chicken with its head cut off."*

Nancy Shelton Norton (she divorced George W. Franklin, Jr., shortly after the war and never remarried) became known as a Union spy and after her sons were killed moved to Knoxville along with her daughter Delaney Jane. There they aided the Union troops by cooking, sewing, and caring for the wounded. To a Mr. Baker, Commander of Pensions, it was written that,

> *"Nancy was one of the most efficient spies in the whole Union Army. Nancy Franklin is perhaps one of the most remarkable women in the war. If one half of the stories told about her are true she must have been a real heroine. In one battle, Nancy directed Union fire by voice from her horse. She yelled to the Union riflemen, 'You are firing too low! You are hitting them in the heels! Raise your fire!'"*

After the war, Nancy and her daughter returned to the Laurel region, where she took up residence with her brother James and his family. Normalcy eventually tried to become re-established in the mountains, and rebuilding and reconstruction began. One of the places heavily damaged by the results of the war was Mars Hill College. The college had been taken over by Rebel forces and was a stronghold and command post for the duration of the war. By the end of the war, all but one building had been destroyed. In 1866, John Ammons (a former Confederate chaplain) was appointed president of the college. Mr. Ammons was able to procure Federal funds to begin rebuilding the college.

Soon Confederate and Union veterans were working side-by-side doing carpentry and masonry. One of the former Confederate soldiers who was hired as a brick mason was a man named Inman. Inman just happened to be in on the raid of the Norton cabin. As a matter of fact, he was the soldier that had shot at Nancy at close range and missed. Inman often talked about his role in the war with other workers, and one day recounted the Norton cabin-burning story. He cheerily stated, *"I took squirrel-aim at her no further off than I am from you at this instant, when I fired. Now I can knock a hawk out of a tree at seventy-five yards, but you won't believe this I didn't nor more than clip a lock of her hair out at the temple. Didn't even draw blood."*

Nearby within earshot were two college students from the Laurel area who knew James Shelton and his sister Nancy. The next day the two students walked twenty miles to the home of James Shelton in Shelton Laurel and told James and Nancy what they had overheard, noting especially how Inman had laughed when he told about missing Nancy when he shot from about twenty feet away. When they had finished, James told the students that he would give them a five dollar gold piece if they would take him back with them and point out the man who had told this story. It was a deal, so the next morning the three of them returned to the college, and the students identified Inman to James. James walked up to the bricklayer and said, *"I heard about that story you was telling, but I'm not sure I have the right of it. Just how did it go?"* Inman laid down his trowel and retold the story about the killings, burning, and taking a shot at the woman, but missing. James interrupted at that point and exclaimed, *"That was my sister. And those boys you killed were my nephews. One had even been named after me."*

James then quickly removed a pistol from his coat and shot Inman at point blank range in the abdomen. He watched as the man fell wiggling among the bricks, then turned and hurried off. Inman died a painful and agonizing death about twenty-two hours later. A posse was formed and searched for James Shelton, but they did not immediately find him. Some said that they looked for James in places they knew he wouldn't be. Eventually, James was captured and jailed in Marshall for the First Degree murder of Inman.

As the time for James Shelton's trial drew closer, the prosecution asked for and was granted a change of venue as they didn't think they could win the totally air-tight case against James in his own county. The case was certainly an open and shut case. There were several witnesses, the victim was unarmed, and Inman even lived long enough, to tell the authorities exactly what had happened. The change of venue ordered that the case be moved to Burnsville, the county seat of Yancey County.

Just before the trial, Nancy saddled her horse and traveled the forty miles to Burnsville by herself, taking little-traveled mountain trails so she wouldn't be seen by anyone.

Finally she got to the trial, tired and ragged, as the prosecution began its case against James. She was the only witness called for the defense. When she took the stand, she recounted the terrible story of the Rebel raid on her home and family, using considerable elegant and dramatic language.   Finally Judge James L. Henry interrupted her dramatic account and judgmentally exclaimed, *"Madam, do you tell us that you told these young boys, one of them not much more than a child, to open fire and kill those men? How could you do that? Why didn't you tell them to live law-abiding Christian lives?"* Nancy's response is probably repeated and memorized in every Shelton and Norton home in Shelton Laurel even today. *"Yes, your honor. I told them to live law-abiding Christian lives. I brought them up to tell the truth and to be honest. But I also told them if you have to die, die like a damned dog, with your teeth in a throat!"*

The jury retired for deliberation, and very shortly returned with the statement, *"We declare that we have found James Shelton NOT GUILTY of the crime of murder."* The jury foreman went on to say, *"It was murder, but a justifiable one."*

 Later in life Nancy lived with her daughter Delaney Jane, who had married Mitchell Tillery Franklin, George

W. Franklin, Jr.'s younger brother. After Nancy helped raise Delaney Jane and Mitchell's children, she went to live with her only remaining son George and his wife Nancy in Greene County, TN. Nancy Shelton Norton Franklin died on January 5, 1905, and is buried alongside her son George and his wife in the Mount Olive Cemetery in the Greystone community of Greene County.

Burial site of Nancy Shelton Norton Franklin in Mount Olive Cemetery, Greene County, Tennessee

Chapter Five
Execution at Mossy Creek:
The Story of William "Bill" Shelton
(1809-1864)

The various ways of the author's kinship to Bill Shelton:

1. Me--- Edd Shelton--- Joe Shelton--- B. E. Shelton--- Riley Shelton---Bill Shelton
2. Me---Edd Shelton---Joe Shelton---Avarinza Hensley---Matilda Shelton---Bill Shelton
3. Me---Edd Shelton---Nellie Hensley---Bevy Hensley*---Nancy Shelton---Bill Shelton
4. Me---Velma King---Woolsey King---George King (Hensley)*---Nancy Shelton---Bill Shelton
5. Me--- Velma King---Woolsey King---Matilda Haire---Nick Haire---Matilda Shelton---Bill Shelton
6. Me---Velma King---Doshia Cutshaw---Ileathy Shelton---Hickman Shelton---James Shelton---Bill Shelton

*Bevy and George were brothers. George changed his name to King later in life to avoid confusion, as he had a first cousin whose name was also George Hensley.

Their mother's first husband was Ellison King, who was killed in the Shelton Laurel Massacre, and George changed his name to "King" in honor of Ellison. Nancy (their mother) married Bill Hensley a few years after Ellison was killed.

As one can see, there are four different ways that Bill Shelton is my great-great-great grandfather, and two different ways that he is my great-great-great-great grandfather. If it were possible to do a comparative analysis of mine and Bill's DNA, I'm sure they would be a virtual match.

William "Bill" Shelton was born in 1809, the second child of David Shelton and Catherine Miller, in the Alleghany section of Shelton Laurel. At the time this area was part of Buncombe County, North Carolina. (Madison County wasn't formed until 1851). David, his brothers, Martin and Roderick, Jr., and their father Roderick, Sr. were the first settlers to establish homesteads in this region, and the name "Shelton Laurel" is in honor of David Shelton. Other children of David and Catherine besides Bill were Nancy (1807), Isaac (1812), Eliphas (1814), Alexander (1815), Molly (1817), Margaret, sometimes called Peggy (1818), David, Jr. (1822), Catherine, sometimes called Katy (1824), Sarah, Sometimes called Sacky (1826), James (1827), John (1829), and Judith, sometimes called Judy (1833). The birth dates in parentheses may be off a year or so. All of these Sheltons' family listings can be found in *The Sheltons*, by Clay Hensley and Zelois Shelton Hensley.

Bill married Cloey Riddle on December 18, 1829, in Yancey County, North Carolina. Their children were James (1828), Matilda (1831), Noah (1834), (Noah was the first of many of Bill's close relatives to be killed in the Civil War), Riley (1836), Nancy (1838), Peter (1841), John (1842), Minerva Jane (1844), Eliphas (1845), Isabel Dansel (1847), Iona (1849), and Montgomery (1852).

Bill Shelton was probably best known in his younger years as being an outstanding bear hunter. In an unpublished manuscript William "Bud" Shelton wrote that his great-uncle Bill *"was a great hunter for wild game, it is said he killed more black bears, here in the Blue Ridge mountains than any other man, before the Civil War."* My father Edd told us the story that once Bill was tracking a bear that he had possibly wounded, and he was carrying his old flintlock rifle across his shoulder. The bear had circled back and was following Bill behind him. By the time he realized the bear was stalking him, it had already begun to charge. Bill didn't have time to turn around and swing his rifle off his shoulder, so he just shot the rifle as it lay across his shoulder, luckily killing the bear as it lunged for him. I have no way of validating this story, but it sure sounds like something that a famous bear hunter could coolly accomplish without panicking.

Bill Shelton was already fifty-two years old when the Civil War began, so I'm sure he didn't think much about choosing a side or serving, but during the summer of 1862, his son Noah was killed while serving with the Union army in Kentucky. Then on January 19, 1863, his brother James, four of his nephews (James, Jr., David, Azariah, and William Shelton), and his son-in-law Ellison King were executed while being held prisoners in what later became known as the Shelton Laurel Massacre. Two days before the massacre there was a skirmish at Bill's farm between members of the Rebel 64th North Carolina regiment and civilian citizens of Shelton Laurel. I'm sure Bill was present and participated in the battle against the Rebels. Many of the local mountain men escaped higher up into the mountains, but fifteen (mostly older men and boys) were taken captive. This is the subject of another story in another chapter.

In the fall of 1863, Knoxville, Tennessee. was taken over by Union forces. Until then, a Union pilot from Carter County Tennessee, Daniel Ellis, guided many mountain men to Kentucky to avoid the Confederate conscription, which became law in April of 1862, and affected men ages eighteen to thirty-five. There were hundreds of men who would rather sneak through the lines and join the Union Army than to be forced to serve in the Confederate Army. After Knoxville was liberated by the Yankees, Mr. Ellis guided men to Knoxville to enlist, and his route took him right through Shelton Laurel. In his book, *Thrilling Adventures of Daniel Ellis*, he states that one of the places that he would make camp was at Bill Shelton's farm. One of the men that he recruited was Peter Shelton, Bill's son. He wrote in his book that Peter was very courageous and was willing to take chances, even with unfavorable odds. At some point, Bill joined the 2nd North Carolina Mounted Volunteers. I don't know if Daniel Ellis recruited him, or if Col. George Kirk from Greene County, Tennessee, signed him up (another possibility was Bill's brother John, who was a captain in the 2nd NCMV, recruited him).

In Bud Shelton's unpublished manuscript, he writes that Bill went to Kentucky and joined the Union Army to escape conscription and was killed in the Battle of Knoxville. I don't think this information is correct because the Conscription Act would not have applied to him (he was too old), and his death date was early May, 1864, eight months after the Rebels gave up the siege of Knoxville. I could certainly imagine Bill having to leave Shelton Laurel to escape the atrocities that the remnants of the 64th and the Home Guards, were inflicting upon the pro-Union citizens who inhabited the area.

The main body of the 64th had been defeated and captured in the battle of Cumberland Gap in early September of 1863, and their main leader, James Keith, had been forced to resign his commission because of his involvement in the Shelton Laurel Massacre (many members of the 64th died at a Union prison camp in Chicago, Illinois, before the war's end).

Bill Shelton was captured at Mossy Creek in Jefferson County, Tennessee., in early May, 1864, and on May 8th was executed along with some other captives by being marched down the railroad a short distance and shot. All of the victims were buried in a common unmarked grave. The rest of the Bill Shelton story is regarding his widow Cloey's attempts to be granted a widow's pension from the government. There was an Act of Congress that was approved on July 14, 1862, that paid eligible widows eight per month and four dollars per month for any child under sixteen years of age. In Cloey's first application for pension, filed on December 8, 1866, she listed Iona (1849), and Montgomery (1852) as dependents eligible for compensation. One of the problems regarding her claim was that Iona was already sixteen years old by July of 1866. Her initial claim was rejected, October 3, 1872, due to not enough evidence that Bill had actually joined the Union army.

Cloey was a persistent woman, and immediately re-applied for pension, with additional evidence supplied in the form of affidavits from former Capt. John Shelton and former Col. George Kirk. The following is the affidavit submitted by Col. Kirk.

"I George W. Kirk late Col. 3rd N.C. Mt. Infry. Certify on oath that I was personal acquainted with William Shelton Sr. late private Co. E 2nd N.C. Mt. Infry. And know the following facts in regard to the death of this said William Shelton. That the said Shelton was captured with others by

the rebels and said Shelton was taken out and shot to death by said Confederates on or about the 14th of May 1864 in Jefferson County, Tenn. That this affiant has frequently passed by the place where said Shelton was killed and where he is still buried. That this affiant has frequently seen men who were present at the time said Shelton was killed and who assisted in the burying of said Shelton and as to the fact of said Wm. Shelton being dead and killed by the enemy on or about the 14th of May 1864. There cannot be the least shadow of a doubt as this affiant was during and since the war been personally acquainted with the family. This affiant has no interest in any claim for pension on account of his death.   Geo. W. Kirk,   Feb. 16th 1871."

John Shelton, who was an officer of the 2nd N. C. Mounted Infantry, and who also was Bill Shelton's younger brother, testified before the Clerk of the Superior Court of Madison County D. L. Davis twice to supply additional information for the pension claim. The following are the contents of these testimonies.

John Shelton Affidavit #1:   "On this the 21st day of March 1874, personally appeared before me _____ of a court of record in and for said county, John Shelton late Leut. Of Company E 2nd N. C. Mt. Infry. And who being duly sworn define and say that William Shelton Sr. a volunteer for the _____ _____ was with this affiant and was serving with the detachment of regular United

States troops, under this affiant at the time he was captured and killed in May 1864 by the rebels. That this affiant had been acquainted with the said Wm. Shelton Sr. for some time, and also said Wm. Shelton Sr. had been in many fights against the rebels with this affiant and at the time of his capture and being killed was serving under this affiant and this affiant has no interest in the claim for pension. John Shelton.   Sworn to and subscribe before me day and date above written, and I certify that John Shelton is a man of truth and honesty and I have no interest in this claim. D. L. Davis, Clerk, Superior Court County of Madison, State of North Carolina."

John Shelton Affidavit #2:   "On this the 27th day of June A. D. 1874 personally appeared before me in the Superior Court for said county John Shelton formerly Lt. Company E 2nd N. C. Mt. Infry. And who being sworn declare and say that he was present at Mossy Creek, Tenn. in May 1864 when Wm. Shelton Sr. was captured by the rebels. That the said Wm. Shelton Sr. was taken up the railroad a short distance and shot to death by the rebels. That this affiant further states that the said Wm. Shelton was there cooperating with United States troops at the time he was captured and killed. That the said Wm. Shelton Sr. was cooperatives with this affiant and under his command at the time he was captured and killed. That the said Shelton had been in several

The author feels the need to point out that there were two William Sheltons in the 2nd N.C. Mounted Infantry, with the younger one being the son of Isaac Shelton, Bill Shelton's brother. People serving with them referred to them as William Sr. and William Jr.: they were uncle-nephew, not father-son. The younger William would be killed along with his father, Isaac, and his uncle, David Shelton Jr. in July of 1864, on top of the Butt Mountain. That story is the focus of another chapter.

Finally, Cloey Shelton's claim for pension was approved January 20, 1875, retroactive to July, 1866. At the time of this writing, the author has not been able to locate the place at Mossy Creek where Bill Shelton was executed, nor have I been able to locate where Cloey Riddle Shelton is buried, and so this ends the story of my great-great-great grandparents.

William "Bill" Shelton, the author's great-great-great grandfather

Government documents regarding Cloey Shelton's application for military widow's pension

WIDOW'S CLAIM FOR PENSION.

State of _North Carolina_
County of _Madison_ } ss.

ON THIS 8th day of _December_ 1886, personally appeared before me, a _Clerk_ ... of a Court of Record in and for the County and State aforesaid, _Cloey Shelton_ a resident of _Laurel_ in the County of _Madison_ and State of _North Carolina_ aged _54_ years, who being duly sworn, makes the following declaration, in order to obtain the Pension provided by the Act of Congress approved **July 14, 1862.** That she is the widow of _William Shelton_ who was a _Private_ in Company _E_ commanded by _Capt. Walker_ in the _2nd_ Regiment of _North Carolina Vol._ in the War of 1861; that her maiden name was _Cloey Shelton_ and that she was married to said _William Shelton_ on or about the _8th_ day of _December_ 1829, at _Laurel_ in the County of _Madison_ and State of _North Carolina_ by _Nathan Woodson_ and that she knows of no record evidence of said marriage _having been burnt up_ ...

SHE FURTHER DECLARES that said _William Shelton_ her husband, died in the service of the United States as aforesaid at _Nashville Tenn._ in the State of _Tennessee_ on or about the _____ day of _May_ 1864, at _Nashville, being taken prisoner by the enemy and killed, or murdered by them_

... She also declares that she has remained a widow ever since the death of said _William Shelton_ and that she has not in any manner been engaged in, or aided or abetted, the rebellion in the United States; and she hereby appoints _B. F. Hyman_ of _Washington D.C._ as her lawful attorney, with power of substitution, and authorizes _him_ to present and prosecute this claim, and to receive her pension certificate. The following are the names, dates of birth and places of residence of all the children of her deceased husband who were under sixteen years of age at the time of his death:

Montgomery Bern April 30th 1852 — Anna Bern Oct 20th 1860, &c.

My Post Office address is _Marshall, Madison Co. N.C._

If mark is made, two witnesses who subscribe here.

Cloes A. Nichols   Cloey + Shelton
M. S. Christy   mark
                                         (Signature of Claimant)

ALSO PERSONALLY APPEARED before me _James M. Candler_ and _George Franklin_ citizens of _Madison_ County, and State of _North Carolina_ to me well known as credible persons, who being duly sworn, declare, that they were present and saw said _Cloey Shelton_ sign her name to the foregoing declaration, and that they have every reason to believe, from the appearance of said applicant, and their acquaintance with her, that she is the identical person she represents herself to be, and know that said deceased recognized said applicant as his lawful wife, and that she was so recognized by the community in which they resided; and that they have no interest, direct or indirect, in the prosecution of this claim.

                          James Candler
(Signature of Witness)   _George Franklin_

WAR OF THE REBELLION.   Act of July 14, 1862, and subsequent acts.

WIDOW'S PENSION.

(ORIGINAL WITH INCREASE.)

Cloa or Cloe Shelton, Widow of

William Shelton Senr   { Rank, Private

{ Company, 8

{ Regiment, 2 NC

Residence of claimant, Madison County, and State of North Carolina

Post office, Marshall

Attorney, T. Het McPherson, Washington DC

Fee, $

No contract, and no material evidence filed since July 6, 1879.

Rate of pension, $ per month, commencing   , 18   , the date

of   , and two dollars per month additional for each child, as follows:

By former marriage.	{ Born, ____ , 18 } { Sixteen, ____ , 18 }	Commencing , 18
	{ Born, ____ , 18 } { Sixteen, ____ , 18 }	" , 18
	{ Born, ____ , 18 } { Sixteen, ____ , 18 }	" , 18
	{ Born, ____ , 18 } { Sixteen, ____ , 18 }	" , 18
	{ Born, ____ , 18 } { Sixteen, ____ , 18 }	" , 18
By last marriage. Montgomery	{ Born, April 26, 1852 } { Sixteen, " 29, 1868 }	" , 18
	{ Born, ____ , 18 } { Sixteen, ____ , 18 }	" , 18
	{ Born, ____ , 18 } { Sixteen, ____ , 18 }	" , 18
	{ Born, ____ , 18 } { Sixteen, ____ , 18 }	" , 18

Payments on all former certificates covering any portion of the same time to be deducted.

Rejected

Admitted, October 3 , 1872 M. Braddee , Examiner.

Approved, Oct. 26 , 1872 . Mo. J. R. adj , Reviewer.

, Chief of Division.

DATES SHOWN BY PAPERS.

Enlistment,	, 18	Widow's app. filed,	Mar 14 , 1867
Muster into rank,	, 18	Claim completed,	not ____ , 18
Discharge,	, 18	Former marriage of soldier,	, 18
Death,	May 8 , 1864	Death of former wife,	, 18
Invalid app. filed,	, 18	Claimant's marriage to soldier,	, 18
Invalid last paid to	, 18		Decem 8 , 1829

Cause of death, "Killed" or Murdered. Place of death, Russellville Tenn

56

WIDOW'S PENSION.
(ORIGINAL WITH INCREASE.)

Elva Shelton   , Widow of

William Shelton Sen.

Rank, *Priv*

Company, *E*

Regiment, *2º NCMtdVols*

No. 7,298

Residence of claimant, *Madison* County, and State of *N. C.*

Post office, *Marshall, Madison Co. N. C.*

Attorney, *L. D. Johnson, Washington DC.*

Atty's, $10.ºº

No contract, and no material evidence filed since July 8, 1870.

Rate of pension, $ *8.ºº* per month, commencing *May 3* , 18 *64*, the date of *soldiers death* , and two dollars per month additional for each child, as follows:

	Born,	18			, 18
	Sixteen,	18	Commencing		, 18
	Born,	18			, 18
	Sixteen,	18	"		, 18
	Born,	18			, 18
My former marriage.	Sixteen,	18	"		, 18
	Born,	18			, 18
	Sixteen,	18	"		, 18
Montgomery	Born, *Apl. 30,* 18 *62*			*July 20* , 18 *66*
	Sixteen, *Apl. 29,* 18 *68*		"	
	Born,	18			, 18
My last marriage.	Sixteen,	18	"		, 18
	Born,	18			, 18
	Sixteen,	18	"		, 18
	Born,	18			, 18
	Fixteen,	18	"		, 18
	Born,	18			, 18
	Sixteen,	18	"		, 18

Payments on all former certificates covering any portion of the same time to be deducted.

Admitted, *Jany 6* , 18 *75*.   *M. D. Pick* , Examiner.

Approved, *January 20* , 18 *75*.   *Mc. Roberts* , Reviewer.

, Chief of Division.

DATES SHOWN BY PAPERS.

Enlistment,	*None*	, 18	Widow's app. filed,	*May 4*	, 18 *67*
Muster into rank,	"	, 18	Claim completed,	*Mar. 27*	, 18 *74*
Discharge,	"	, 18	Former marriage of soldier,	*None*	, 18
Death,	*May 3*	, 18 *64*.	Death of former wife,	"	, 18
Invalid app. filed,	*None*	, 18	Claimant's marriage to soldier,	*Dec 18, 18* *29*	
Invalid last paid to,	"	, 18			, 18

CAUSE OF DEATH, *Murdered while a prisoner* PLACE OF DEATH, *Russellville, Tenn.*

No. 167775

North Carolina

Alea Shelton

WIDOW OF

William Shelton

Rank _______ Priv _______

Regt _______ 2 N. C. Art. Vol.

Raleigh _______ Agency

Rate per Month $8

Commencing _______ 3 May 1864

Additional sum of $2 per Month for each of
the following children, until arriving of the age of
16 years, commencing _______ 25 July 1866

Montgomery 29 April 1868

Certificate dated _______ 3 Feby 1875

Sent to _______ L. A. D. Shaw
Alea

Act 14th July, 1862.

Chapter Six
Ambush at Cold Spring
The Story of David Shelton, Junior
(1822-1864)

The author's kinship to David Shelton, Jr.

Me—Velma King—Doshia Cutshaw—Ileathy Shelton—Kindness Shelton—David Shelton, Jr.

David Shelton, Jr. is my great-great-great grandfather.

David Shelton, Jr.'s parents were David Shelton and Catherine Miller. For a listing of his siblings, refer to "The Story of William (Bill) Shelton". David, Jr. lived his childhood and teenaged life in the Alleghany region of Shelton Laurel. This area was originally part of Buncombe County, but in 1833, became part of Yancey County. Then in 1851, Shelton Laurel became and is still today part of Madison County.

On March 9, 1842, David, Jr. and Elizabeth Gosnell were married by Justice of the Peace Nealey Tweed. Elizabeth had been born in South Carolina in 1824, and I do not know the details of how they met. David, Jr. and Elizabeth had the following children: Jane (1844), Kindness (1845), Judith (1846), Green Berry (1850), William Riley (1852), Catherine (1854), and Omie

(1862). All of these Sheltons' family listings can be found in *The Sheltons*, by Clay Hensley and Zelois Shelton Hensley.

When the Civil War began David, Jr., like most other men of the Laurel region, just wanted to be left alone. On January 19, 1863, the Shelton Laurel Massacre occurred, and David, Jr. lost several close kinfolks (a brother and four nephews). Shortly after the 2nd North Carolina Mounted Volunteers (Union) were formed David, Jr., his nephew William (his brother, Issac's son) and some more of his close relatives went to Warm Springs (now called Hot Springs) and enlisted on September 1, 1863. David Jr. and William evidently didn't like army life and within a couple of months, both had deserted and had gone back home to Shelton Laurel. There they hid out from the remnants of the 64th Confederate forces and the Home Guards of the Confederates, who were combing the area for anyone they could conscript. Meanwhile Col. George Kirk and the Union 2nd went to Knoxville to await orders.

Col. Kirk must have gotten bored by the way the war was going and so he devised a daring plan to travel over one hundred miles behind enemy lines and attack Camp Vance at Morganton, North Carolina. There he hoped to capture the Confederate conscripts being trained there, destroy or seize arms and munitions being stored there, capture a locomotive and run down to Saulisbury, North Carolina and liberate Union prisoners being held there, and burn a bridge or two in the process. He realized that he would need more men than what he had to accomplish this mission, so he sent some of his officers out to recruit deserters and others. One of his officers was Lt. John Shelton, David Jr.'s younger brother. John went back to Shelton Laurel and convinced David Jr. and William to return to the unit and go on the Camp Vance mission, with the promise that each man that participated would be given a horse if the mission was successful. Col. Kirk got the authority to carry out the mission from Gen. Schofield, and on June 13, 1864, left Morristown, Tennessee. with about 130 men, including about a dozen Cherokees that had deserted Thomas' Legion. At Greeneville, Tennessee, they were met by around sixty men from Madison County who had been gathered up by Lt. John Shelton. All of the men were on foot, carrying their rations, arms, and ammunition on their shoulders. Col. Kirk had armed his regiment well, with most of the men carrying Spencer lever-action repeater rifles. These guns could shoot eight rounds in a matter of seconds, far out-performing the single-shot muskets with which the Rebels were equipped.

Col. Kirk and his troops passed through to the North Carolina line undetected. In Carter County, Tennessee, they picked up a guide and were able to pass through Avery and Burke County, North Carolina, without any resistance. At dawn on June 28, 1864 they reached the Conscript camp at Berry's Mill Pond. There they formed a line of battle, and Kirk emerged from the woods under a flag of truce and demanded the surrender of the entire camp in ten minutes. The camp's commandant, Maj. McClean, was mysteriously absent. Therefore, the camp's leading officer was a lieutenant by the name of Bullock, who agreed to surrender. The Union troops then proceeded to destroy one locomotive, three cars, 1,200 small arms with ammunition, and 3,000 bushels of corn. Kirk and his men captured 279 prisoners, (132 were taken back to Knoxville), and forty-eight horses and mules. He also got forty new recruits for his regiment (Rebel soldiers who suddenly decided they wanted to become Yankees).

While the militia and Home Guards were gathering to try to thwart the capture, one of Kirk's scouts was killed at Hunting Creek about one half mile from Morganton by Dr. R. C. Pearson, a leading citizen of the town. The Union soldier who was killed was Hack Norton. Norton was David Shelton Jr.'s nephew (his sister Nancy's son). When Col. Kirk heard that there were several columns of Rebels going to converge on Morganton, he decided not to attempt to go to Saulisbury to free Union prisoners, nor was he able to burn the bridge over the Yadkin River. He immediately headed west. Late in the day, a force of Rebels caught up with them at Brown's Mountain and they formed a line of fire for the ensuing battle.

Kirk positioned about twenty prisoners taken from Camp Vance in front of the line. When the Rebels started firing, they killed and wounded some of the prisoners. Col. Kirk was heard shouting, *"Look at the damned fools, shooting their own men!"* Afterwards the Rebels withdrew, and Kirk's entire regiment escaped. The Union casualties were one killed (Norton), one mortally wounded, and five (including Col. Kirk, who took a bullet in the arm) wounded. When Kirk got back to Knoxville in early July, he was hailed a hero. The total distance that the regiment had traveled was over two hundred miles, and Kirk even received congratulatory notes from Gens. Sherman and Stoneman.

Now here is the tragic part of the story. On or about July 3, 1864, when Kirk's regiment passed close by Shelton Laurel on the way back to Knoxville, David Shelton, Jr., William Shelton, Ephraim Hensley, and possibly seven or eight other soldiers from the Laurel region left the regiment and went to the top of the Butt Mountain and hid out for several days in an old shack. Whether they were given leave or went AWOL will be addressed later. The band of soldiers were joined later by at least three civilians, two older men and one young teenager. For the next couple of weeks this group plundered and stole provisions from local homesteads, thinking any Rebel force that might be in the area wouldn't find their hideout. Upon hearing about the presence of the group, a Rebel detachment was sent from Warm Springs with orders to find and defeat the group.

Early on the morning of July 19, 1864, fourteen-year old Millard Haire (my great-grandmother Avarinza's half-brother and my great-great grandfather Nick Haire's full brother) woke up first, and thought he would have a little fun with the other sleeping men. He climbed up onto an old chestnut stump and started crowing like a rooster. Little did he know that the Rebel detachment had discovered their hideout and had the place surrounded. While Millard Haire was in the middle of his rooster crow, a Rebel sharpshooter blew him backwards off the stump, killing him instantly. The sleeping men in the shack woke up suddenly, ran out to see what the shooting was all about, and were met by a deadly hail of gunfire. David Shelton, Jr. and William Shelton were killed and several of the soldiers were wounded, including Ephraim Hensley. Two older civilians, Isaac Shelton, Sr. (William Shelton's father and David, Jr.'s older brother), and Hampton Burgess, Sr. tried to escape by running away but the ensuing Rebels caught up with them about a fourth of a mile out the trail (now the Appalachian Trail) and shot them dead. Three of the men escaped unharmed, and Ephraim Hensley hid in a laurel thicket motionless and watched the whole ordeal. He was shot in the lower back, but survived the wound and lived until 1916.

The source of this story mainly comes from his eyewitness account. The Rebels took five of the wounded as prisoners and marched them back to their headquarters at Warm Springs. The total casualty count for the Union group was five killed and six wounded. Shortly after the Rebels left, family members went to the top of the Butt Mountain and buried David, William, and Millard in a common grave. Hampton Burgess, Sr. and Isaac Shelton, Sr. were buried close to where they were killed in unmarked graves. In 1915, military markers were placed at the head and foot of the grave for David and William.

No such markers were provided for Millard Haire, Hampton Burgess, Sr., or Isaac Shelton, Sr. because they had not been in the army. Now hundreds of hikers and backpackers pass by the markers every year on the Appalachian Trail. The markers have the names "William Shelton" and "David Shelton" along with their unit "Company E, 2nd N. C. Inf." I often wonder if these hikers from all over the world that see these markers ever stop and think, *"I wonder what the story behind these graves is?"*

The rest of the story is about my great-great-great grandmother Elizabeth. David Shelton, Jr.'s death left her a widow with four children still at home to provide for. In November of 1868, she applied for and was granted a government pension, based solely on an affidavit submitted by her brother-in-law, former Capt. John Shelton. A few months later she began applying for an increase in pension, which led to a lengthy investigation by Special Agent G. H. Ragsdale of the Pension Claims office in Washington, D. C. He took several affidavits from individuals. The following is the affidavit submitted by John Shelton on April 24, 1877:

"Stated that he was a member of Company "E" 2nd NC Mtd Infantry and that David Shelton was his brother. Stated that said brother left the company without leave at Cumberland Gap about Dec. 1, 1863. John Shelton was sent home soon after that time to gather up a number of deserters from the company. John remained at home until sometime in May and then took about 20 members of the company through to Knoxville and among them was his brother David. They were ordered to report to George Kirk of the 3rd NC Vols. to make a raid under Kirk to Morganton, NC. John states he commanded these men on said raid and his brother accompanied

the expedition to Morganton and back as far as his home in Madison Co. NC. John said he gave his brother verbal leave to stop and rest. He had given out on account of an old wound (cut of an axe). John thinks that Major Kirk also gave David verbal permission to stop. This was the last of June or the first of July, and while home on the 19th of July 1864, David Shelton was captured by the enemy and killed."

The following statement tells a very different story. Here is an affidavit of J. M. Sprinkle to Special Agent G. Ragsdale given on May 19, 1877:

"J. M. Sprinkle states he was a Lieutenant in Co. "C" 3rd Mtd Infantry and was with Col. G. W. Kirk on the Camp Vance raid. That on the return from Camp Vance the affiant, J. M. Sprinkle endeavored to get permission to stop one night at home promising to be on hand promptly the next morning. That the command was then passing near his home and afterward passed up Shelton Laurel. That Kirk replied to affiant's request that he could not spare a man. That they had more prisoners than they had men to guard them, and more horses to take care of than men to look after them. Affiant insisted on stopping at home overnight and Kirk remarked that if affiant was allowed to stop others would want to stop and he was afraid they would not come back. That he finally gave affiant to understand that if he would drop out without anyone knowing it and be back

promptly next morning it would be alright. That affiant, afterward, considering the danger of stopping within the rebel lines did not leave the command. They were expecting to be attacked at any moment. That in passing up Laurel a number of the men who lived there dropped out against said Kirk's orders and Kirk swore he would have them shot and made a great fuss about men leaving him at such a time. That affiant had no acquaintance with David Shelton and does not know about his having a sore foot, but he is confident that if David Shelton was along he did not have permission to stop at home within the rebel lines because he was needed badly, and being mounted he was not disabled from marching on account of a sore foot. That no permission was given to anyone to stop except perhaps in the same way permission was given to affiant. If Shelton had stopped on this kind of permission he would have had to promise to be on hand the next morning."

The following is an affidavit that was provided to Special Agent Ragsdale from Roderick Shelton on June 15, 1877. Roderick was Martin Shelton's son and a first cousin of David Shelton, Jr.:

"Roderick states he is 56 years old and was a member of Co. "E" 2nd NC Mtd. Infantry from its organization to muster out. That he was elected 2nd Lt. at first by the men but the company was not full and he was not commissioned until Sept.,

1864. That he acted as Lt. all the time and commanded the company longer than anyone else. That he well remembers David Shelton who was a member of the company. That said David Shelton deserted and did duty with the company but a very short time. That he has no knowledge of David being with the 3rd NC since that regiment was not in existence until after David Shelton left. Roderick believes that David was on the Camp Vance raid but dropped out on the return and was shortly killed near Cold Spring while hiding out with a number of men who had been engaged in plundering. He states that David was not with any command at that time but was with other deserters."

After Special Agent Ragsdale's investigation was completed, he filed the following final report to the Honorable J. H. Bentley, Commissioner of Pensions, Washington D. C.:

"Sir, I have the honor to report the results of an investigation made in case No. 158257 of Elizabeth Shelton, widow of David Shelton, Private, Co. "E" 2nd NC Mtd. Infantry. This man enlisted in said company and remained with it long enough to draw clothing and then deserted. There is no enlistment papers or muster in roll showing that this man was ever in the service. The records have been made to include his name as a member of Co. "E" 2nd NC Mtd. Infantry. (Due to collaborated testimony of his enlistment

and service). He went with Kirk on the raid to Camp Vance N. C. because everyone who went on this raid was promised a horse. On the return from this raid the expedition passed up Laurel by the home of said Shelton which was behind enemy lines.

"This man and a number of others of the same class fell out and refused to go any further. They found other associates with whom they had been laying out. They made their hiding place on Butt Mountain and supposed the rebels could not find them and could not get up on the mountain even if their hiding place was known. From this location they made raids and pressed whatever property they could find. The rebels regarded them as a band of robbers and were anxious to find them. They finally succeeded in slipping up on the party and almost annihilated it. Five men were killed and a number was wounded. David Shelton was killed. This claim that he had permission to fall out and rest two or three days—if this was true, it would not helped the matter as he stopped within the rebel lines. That he did not have permission to fall out is apparent from the affidavits herewith from Sprinkle and from the facts of the case.

"More prisoners had been captured than Kirk had men and at the same time a rebel command was following up and a fight was expected at any moment. It is not reasonable to suppose that under such circumstances Kirk went to excusing

men to stop at home within the rebel lines. William Shelton, David Shelton, Ezekiel Jones, Ephraim Hensley and others say they had permission to stop. The widows of two of them have been pensioned and one of them is receiving an invalid pension and the other one is a claimant. They were deserters before they went on this raid and all but one was shot soon after they fell out of the command and stopped at home. They were not with any command at the time they were shot but were with other men who were known as common robbers.

"This man David Shelton was a brother to John Shelton who had command of the men from the 2nd NC Mtd. Infantry who were placed on detachment service with Col. Kirk. I submit his affidavit admitting that his said brother was killed while at home and while absent from the command. The previous claim was allowed on the testimony made by him. The pensioner makes the same admission. The attorney W. W. Rollins received one half of the first payment or about $600 for his services and John Shelton received $50 for what assistance he rendered. The command was on the Camp Vance raid about one month and this is all the service David Shelton did with the 2nd NC and he deserted six months before an effort was made to recruit the 3rd NC."

Special Agent Ragsdale's investigation led to the curtailment of Elizabeth Shelton's pension payments on

September 4, 1877. She continually tried to get the pension reinstated, but to no avail. The last time she tried was in June of 1898. She was living with her daughter Catherine and her husband in Flag Pond, TN. at the time. By 1900, she had moved back to Shelton Laurel and was living with another daughter (Jane) and her husband. Elizabeth Gosnell Shelton died shortly after 1900, and I have not been able to locate where she is buried.

Whether David Shelton, Jr. and his nephew William had written or verbal permission to leave the regiment, or whether they were AWOL doesn't matter now. They were both gunned down while still in their prime, and their families had to face life without them. As David's great-great-great grandson, it would be nice to think he had permission to fall out and rest an old foot injury. Kirk's raid had captured only 48 horses and mules, so there's no way all of the men could have been mounted. However, one of the inbred characteristics of the Sheltons is our stubbornness, so I certainly accept that it is entirely likely that he could have been AWOL. The Federal government certainly recognized the men's service in the Union army by granting them military headstones in 1915, and their deaths were ultimately the result of their service in the participation of the highly successful Camp Vance raid. I am extremely proud of all of my ancestors and realize the tremendous hardships placed upon them and their families during the tragic time in our history known as the War Between the States.

Military-issued headstones for David Shelton, Jr. and William Shelton, located 5.2 miles south of Devil's Fork Gap on the Appalachian Trail

Ileathy Shelton Cutshaw (granddaughter of David Shelton, Jr.) and her family. Ileathy and Gideon Cutshaw are the author's great-grandparents.

(No. 16.)

Department of the Interior,
PENSION OFFICE.

Nov 20, 1868

Sir:

You are respectfully requested to furnish official evidence of the enrollment, muster, service, duty, and cause of death of _David Shelton_ _____, who was a _Priv_ in Co. "C", 2 Regiment of _N. C. Mtd._ Vol., reported died _July 19_, 1864, _Cold Springs Tenn_.

If the above name is not found on the Rolls of said Company, will you so state, and report as to enrollment, &c., in the case of any man bearing a similar name whom you have good reason for believing to be the soldier inquired for. When the Rolls show him to have been a Prisoner of War, let that fact be reported.

____

____

Please attach this Circular to your report, and return the same to this Office.

No. 446.096,

Respectfully, yours,

Chas. C. Cox.
Commissioner

The Adjutant General, U. S. A.,
Washington, D. C.

(No. 14.)

Department of the Interior.

PENSION OFFICE.

Nov 20, 1868.

Sir:

You are respectfully requested to furnish official evidence of the date and cause of death of _David Shelton_, who was a _Priv_ in Co. _"E"_, _U_ Regiment of _N. C. Mtd Vol_ Volunteers, who is reported to have died at _Cedar Spring Town_ on the _19_ day of _July_, 1864, of _______

If the soldier died in hospital, state also at what date he was admitted to the same and for what he was treated.

Please attach this Circular to your report, and return the same to this Office.

No. _16.096._

Respectfully, &c.,

Chris Cox.

Commissioner.

Surgeon Gen'l, U. S. A.

Adjutant General's Office,
Washington, D. C.
Dec'r 6th 186_

Sir:

I have the honor to acknowledge the receipt from your Office of application for Pension No. _Shh........_, and to return it herewith, with such information as is furnished by the files of this Office.

It appears from the Rolls on file in this Office, that _Dawson Shelton_ was enrolled on the _1st_ day of _Sept._, 1863, at _Laurel B_ in Co. _E_, _1st_ Regiment of _North Carolina Volunteers_, to serve _3_ years, or during the war, and mustered into service as a _private_ on the _1st_ day of _Sept._ 186_3_, at _Knoxville_, in Co. _E_, _1st_ Regiment of _North Carolina_ Volunteers, to serve _3_ years, or during the war. On the Muster Roll of Co. _E_ of that Regiment, for the month of _October_, August 16th 186_5_, he is reported as _Corporal_, mustered out with the company at that date.

I am, Sir, very respectfully,
Your obedient servant,

[signature]
Assistant Adjutant General.

The Commissioner of Pensions,
Washington, D. C.

Declaration of Pensioner for Restoration to the Rolls, under Section 4718 Revised Statutes and Act of March 3, 1879.

STATE OF _North Carolina_, COUNTY OF _Madison_, ss:

On this _3"_ day of _May_ A. D., one thousand eight hundred and eighty-_seven_ personally appeared before _a Clerk Superior Court_ the same being a **Court of Record**, within and for the county and State aforesaid, _Elizabeth Shelton_ aged _57_ years, who being duly sworn according to law, makes the following declaration, asking to be restored to the pension-rolls: That I am the identical _Elizabeth Shelton_ who was pensioned on the rolls of the agency at _Knoxville Tenn._, and whose pension-certificate No. _15-8257_, is herewith returned; that I was last paid at said agency to the _Fourth_ day of _June_ 1877; that I have since resided as follows: _at Flag Pond, Greene County Tennessee_

That I have not claimed pension since the date above given for the following reason: _That I was suspended by order of the Commissioner of Pensions_

and that I _am_ still laboring under the disability for which I was pensioned

that I hereby constitute and appoint with full powers of substitution and revocation, _R. A. Cummings of Marshall N.C._ my attorney to prosecute the above claim; that my residence is at No. ___ in ___ street, in the ___ of ___, county of _Greene_, State of _Tennessee_, and that my post office address is _Flag Pond_.

Stephen Roberts
C W Sweet

Elizabeth X Shelton
mark

Also personally appeared _Stephen Roberts_, residing at No. ___ in _Main_ street, in _Marshall_, and _C. W. Sweet_ residing at No. ___ in _Main_ street, in _Marshall_, persons whom I certify to be respectable and entitled to credit, and who, being by me duly sworn, say that they were present and saw _Elizabeth Shelton_ the claimant, sign name (make her mark) to the foregoing declaration; that they have every reason to believe, from the appearance of said claimant and their acquaintance with her that she is the identical person she represents herself to be; and that they have no interest in the prosecution of this claim.

Stephen Roberts
C W Sweet

Sworn to and subscribed before me this _3"_ day of _May_ A. D. 1879 and I hereby certify that the contents of the above declaration, &c., were fully made known and explained to the applicant and witness before swearing, including the words ___ erased, and the words ___ added; and that I have no interest, direct, or indirect, in the prosecution of this claim.

Jno R Hardwicke

Clerk S C

1. Here state the place at which the applicant has resided.
2. Here state specifically the reasons why pension has ceased to be paid.
3. Here describe the disability for which restoration is claimed, and state (if no disability) whether or not applicant has re-entered since last pension payment; and, if so, give date, company, and regiment, and date of final discharge. If a widow or mother, state whether remarried, or, if remarried, give date.

[Act of June 27, 1890.]

Widow's Declaration for Pension or Increase of Pension.

To be Executed Before a Court of Record or Some Officer Thereof Having Custody of its Seal.

STATE OF _Tennessee_, COUNTY OF _Macon_.

On this _23_ day of _July_ A. D., one thousand eight hundred and ninety, personally appeared before me _C Clark_, of the _County_ court, a court of record within and for the County and State aforesaid, _Elizabeth Shelton_ aged _68_ years, a resident of the _______ of _Briggs_, County of _Macon_, State of _Tennessee_, who, being duly sworn according to law, makes the following declaration in order to obtain the Pension provided by Act of Congress June 27, 1890, granting pension to widows: That she is the widow of _David Shelton_ who enlisted under the name of _David Shelton_ at _______ on the _1_ day of _Sept_ 1863 in Co. "E" 2nd Regt N. C. Mt. Inf. in the war of the rebellion and served at least ninety days, who was ~~discharged at~~ _Killed_ and died on the _______ day of _July_ , 1864. That she is without other means of support than her daily labor. That she was married under the name of _Elizabeth Godwin_ to said _David Shelton_ on the _______ day of _______, 18__, by _Nealy Travis Esq_ at _Living Chandler_, there being no legal barrier to said marriage _______

[If there was a former marriage of claimant or her husband, state it here and here described.]

That she has to present date remained his widow; that the following are the names and dates of birth of all his legitimate children yet surviving who are under sixteen years of age, viz.:

_______ born _______, 18__	_______ born _______, 18__
_______ born _______, 18__	_______ born _______, 18__
_______ born _______, 18__	_______ born _______, 18__

That she has heretofore applied for pension and the number of her former application is _______

She hereby appoints with full power of substitution and revocation,

W. E. F. MILBURN, OF GREENEVILLE, TENN.,

her true and lawful attorney to prosecute her claim, _and directs a fee of ten dollars to be paid for his services_

That her post-office address is _Briggs_, County of _Macon_, State of _Tennessee_.

Joseph M. Ray
B L Briggs
[Two persons who can write.]

                                                    her
                                            Elizabeth ✕ Shelton
                                                   mark
                                            [Claimant sign here.]

DECLARATION FOR RESTORATION TO THE PENSION ROLL.

State of Tennessee, County of Unicoi, ss:

On the 30th day of May, A. D. one thousand eight hundred and ninety-eight,
personally appeared before me, John B. Sams, Dep. for the County Court Clerk, a Court of
RECORD within and for the County and State aforesaid, Elizabeth Shelton,
aged 83, years, who, being duly sworn according to law, makes the following declaration asking to be restored
to the pension roll: That I am the identical Elizabeth Shelton
who was pensioned on the rolls of the Agency at Knoxville Tennessee, and whose pension
certificate No. 158257, is herewith returned; and that I was paid last at said agency to the 4 day of
September at 77 that I since resided as follows: at White Rock
Madison County N.C. from Sept 4 to 1892 and
from 1892 at Flag Pond Unicoi Co. Tenn for
in 1897 to the present date.

That I have not claimed pension since the date above given for the following reasons: That one Special
Examiner by the name of Rosebill, or Rosedale
caused my pension to be stopped, being a poor
woman living in the mountains I did not know my
rights under the law.

and that I Claimant my husband was killed
while on detached service in line of duty while
on return from the capture of Camp Vance
North Carolina under command of Col. Geo.
W. Kirk, that I hereby appoint, with full power of substitution and revocation,
H. E. F. Milburn of Greeneville Tennessee
my attorney to prosecute the above claim; that my residence is in Flag Pond (Unicoi Co)
in the County of Unicoi and State of Tennessee, and
my Postoffice address is Flag Pond, Unicoi County Tenn.

J. M. Ray   Elizabeth her X Shelton
James Heasley   mark

Also personally appeared J. M. Ray, James Heasley and ___ Briggs
whom I certify to be respectable and entitled to
credit, and who, being by me duly sworn, say that they were present and saw Elizabeth Shelton
the claimant, sign name (or make mark) to the foregoing declaration; that they have every reason to believe from the
appearance of said claimant and their acquaintance with her that she is the identical person she represents herself
to be; and that they have no interest in the prosecution of this claim.

J. M. Ray

S. *Brief for Restoration*   WIDOW'S PENSION.

Dis. Cert # 155,257

Claimant: Elizabeth Shelton   Soldier: David Shelton Sr.

P.O.: Flag Pond   Rank: Priv.   Co. E

County: Union   State: Tenn.   Regiment: 2 N.C. Vol Mtd Inf

Rate, $______ per month, commencing ______ 18___, and ______

and two dollars a month additional for each child, as follows:

Payments on all former certificates covering any portion of same time to be deducted.

All pension to terminate ______ 18___, date of ______

REJECTED
Aug. 99. 98

RECOGNIZED ATTORNEY:

Name: W C F Milburn   Fee $______ Agent ______ to pay.

P.O.: Greeneville Tenn   Articles filed ______ 18___

APPROVALS:

Submitted for Reject   July 1   1898,   Signed J. C.   Examiner.

Approved for Rejection, on the ground that the soldier was not in the line of duty when killed due to ______
(See Spl Exr Ragsdales report)
______ which has been legally accepted,

July 30   1898 W. F. Pherson, Legal Reviewer.   ______ 18___, Medical Reviewer.

______ Re-Reviewer.   ______ Medical Referee.

IMPORTANT DATES:

Enlisted ______ Sept 1 ______ 1863   Invalid application filed ______ None, 18___

Reentered ______ 18___ .   Invalid last paid to ______ 18___,

Discharged ______ 18___ .   Former marriage of soldier ______ None, 18___ .

Died ______ July 19 ______ 1864   Death of former wife ______ None, 18___ .

Declaration filed 2nd Oct 3 ______ 1865   Claimant's marriage to soldier ______ Mch 9, 1840
June 6 ______ 1865

Chapter Seven
The Confederate of the Family:
The Story of Bill Hensley (1833-1925)

The ways of the author's kinship to William "Bill" Hensley

1. Me---Edd Shelton---Nellie Hensley---Bevy Hensley---Bill Hensley
2. Me---Velma King---Woolsey King---George King (Hensley)---Bill Hensley

Bill Hensley is my great-great grandfather two different ways.

Bill Hensley's parents were Charles Hensley and Rhoda Franklin. Other children of Charles and Rhoda besides Bill were Lucinda (1822) (wife of Nealey Tweed), Beverly (1825), John (1826) (the author's great-great grandfather from Avarinza Hensley's branch), George (1827), Wesley (1831), Margaret (1840), and Ephraim (1841) (Ephraim was wounded in the ambush on Cold Spring Mountain July 19th, 1864). All of these Hensleys' family listings can be found in *The Sheltons,* by Clay Hensley and Zelois Shelton Hensley.

There are several conflicting theories concerning the origin of Bill's parents. It is generally agreed that Rhoda Franklin was the daughter of Solomon Stanton and Molly (or perhaps Mary) Stevens Franklin. Molly supposedly was a full blooded Cherokee whose Indian name was *Glumdalclitch*. (This is actually a name found in the book *Gulliver's Travels*, by Jonathon Swift. The name was probably provided by some white trader instead of some Cherokee Indian brave). Other children of Molly besides Rhoda (1799) was William (1797), Duck (1799) (Duck may have been Rhoda's twin; later in life Duck went by Shelton instead of Franklin) and George Washington (Rock) (1801). There is also a theory that Rhoda and Duck were illegitimate twin children of Roderick Shelton, Sr. and a woman named Mary Franklin. (Mary Franklin and Molly Stevens Franklin may be one in the same). The theories concerning Charles are as follows:

Theory #1: Charles Hensley (1796) was the son of Colbert Hensley (mother not identified). Other siblings of Charles were Hickman, John, and Amos. Colbert Hensley's parents were Robert Hensley and a Chickasaw Indian woman (a descendant of one of the half-breed Colbert Chiefs, who were sons of a white trader named James Colbert). Robert is supposedly the first Hensley resident of Shelton Laurel. Robert's father was Robert Hensley of Henry County, Virginia (1783 Henry County, Virginia. Tax list).

Theory #2: Charles Hensley was the son of John Hensley and step-mother Martha Hensley. John Hensley appears in the 1790 Burke County, North Carolina census, and the 1784 Henry County, Virginia. Tax list.

Theory #3: Charles Hensley (1796) was raised by a Hensley family after being left on their doorstep as an infant. His father was a Bennett, and his mother was a full-blooded Cherokee Indian woman.

I'll leave it up to the reader to do his or her own research in deciding which theory is correct as this author has no clue.

Bill Hensley married Polly Dudley in 1853. They had six children during the next eight years. The names and the approximate birth dates are as follows: Nealey (1854), Waitsel Avery (1855), Thompson (1858), Rhoda (1859), Eliza (1860), and Solomon (1861). Polly was a domineering woman, and Bill lost his love for her. It's unfortunate that he had fathered six children with her. When she refused to grant him a divorce, he started looking for another way out. On April 12, 1861, shots were fired on Fort Sumter, signaling the beginning of the Civil War. On April 29th, Bill went to Marshall and joined the 6th North Carolina Infantry Volunteers, a Confederate regiment. He was enlisted by Capt. Peek, a cousin of Lawrence Allen, a future colonel of the infamous 64th N. C. Confederate regiment.

One mountain soldier remarked later that, *"when the war came along, I felt mighty southern."* Bill didn't feel "mighty southern", he just wanted to be away from Polly. Bill enlisted as a fifer, so I guess he thought that it would be fairly easy duty to march around playing a fife all day.

However, he eventually became a rifle-bearing private. The first action that the 6th saw was the Battle of Cheat Mountain in September of 1861. In November of 1861, the 6th became the 16th North Carolina Infantry, which consisted of over 2,700 men in the following companies; A (Jackson County) (this company was transferred to and became Company A of Thomas' Legion in May 1862) B; (Madison county; 110 men, one of which was Bill Hensley), C (Yancey County), D (Rutherford County) E (Burke County), F (Buncombe County), G (Rutherford County), H (Macon County), I (Henderson County), K (Polk County), L (Haywood County) (this company was transferred to and became Company E of Thomas' Legion in May 1862), M (Gaston County), and N (Rutherford county).

The 16th originally was known as "Burke's Tigers," and later became part of Hampton's Brigade, Whiting's Division of the Army of Northern Virginia, led by none other than Gen. Robert E. Lee. Major campaigns that Bill Hensley participated in were Seven Pines (May 31, 1862), Seven Days Battle (the Peninsular Campaign) (July 1862), Second Manassas (August 28-30, 1862), Sharpsburg/Antietam (September 1862), and Fredericksburg (December 1862). On February 25, 1863, Bill was injured (I have not been able to find out the type or the extent of his injury) and detailed to Receiving and Wayside Hospital (General Hospital No. 9), Richmond, Virginia. On March 25, 1863 he was assigned to Camp Winder Hospital in Richmond to serve as a guard, as he was physically unable to return to the 16th.

Continuing with following the 16th, other campaigns were Chancellorsville (April 1863), Gettysburg (July 1-3, 1863), Wilderness (May 5-7, 1864), Siege of Petersburg (June 1864 until March 1865), and Appomattox (April 9, 1865). Of the 2,714 men who began with the 16th in 1861, there were 82 enlisted men and 13 officers that were left to surrender at Appomattox.

The Camp Winder Hospital in Richmond became the largest hospital in the Confederacy, and with the wounded of Chancellorsville and Gettysburg pouring in, it became very crowded while Bill Hensley was there. The following is a letter written by one of the guards on duty at the hospital to the *Richmond Whig*, May 21, 1863.

> *"Dear Sir; I am detailed for light hospital duty by Gen. Lee, on account of disability for field service, but upon coming to this camp was put on the guard. I have been here since the 1st of March, and on all occasions have confined myself to the rules and regulations of the place. However, there is one thing I cannot conform to, I cannot be content with short rations, when full allowances are drawn from the commissary for me. You do not allow it and I think, in justice to myself and comrades you should know something about it. This is an imposition, not only to the soldier, but on the government. I hope you will be pleased to enquire why our rations are SOLD by this gentleman in gold lace, when at no time since I have been here have I had enough to eat. Very*

respectfully, your obedient serv't, JAMES WADE, Co. G 14th La. Vol."

Another soldier from Alabama described that Camp Winder Hospital was *"the nastiest place I ever saw in my life"*. Another opinion of the conditions at the hospital appeared in the May 28, 1863 edition of the *Richmond Sentinel.*

> *"In the army much has been said of the ill treatment at this hospital, but if you are ever sent here for the recovery of your health, you may rest assured that you will be well cared for, as the kind hearted ladies at this division (No. 4) are very attentive to their respective duties; and as long as they are able to attend to the sick, and visit their wards with nourishment suitable for your diet, you may rest assured that you will be speedily restored to health, and again ready for duty. J. B. S. Co. A 24th Va. Vols."*

As one can see from these letters, there were varying opinions on the conditions at Camp Winder. Bill Hensley was never able to return to his unit, and on August 31, 1863, was discharged from Camp Winder and the Confederate army. He was paid $151.65 for pay, clothing, and transportation of 556 miles back to Marshall, North Carolina. Upon returning home Bill found that he had the same problem as when he left. Polly still would not grant him a divorce. The difference was that the woman that he was truly in love with was now a widow and available.

Nancy Shelton King's husband Ellison had been executed in the Shelton Laurel Massacre on January 19, 1863. Bill and Nancy began living together, and by 1865, started having children of their own. The following are the children of Bill Hensley and Nancy Shelton King: George (1865), Thomas Jefferson (1868), Burgess (1869), Bevy (1872), twins Abbie and Benjamin (1876) (Abbie died as an infant), and Mattie (1878). Polly eventually agreed to a divorce, and Bill and Nancy were married. Bill's father-in-law Bill Shelton was in the Union army, as well as his younger brother Ephraim. I have found absolutely no accounts where Bill was bothered or harassed because he was a Confederate veteran, and I also have found nothing indicating that he was bothered by remnants of the 64th N. C. Confederates serving as Home Guards. Bill Hensley died in 1925, living to a ripe old age of 92. He and his wife Nancy Shelton Hensley are buried side-by-side in the Union Chapel Cemetery in the Horse Creek area of Greene County, Tennessee.

Bill and Nancy Shelton Hensley with son Ben

Burial site of Bill and Nancy Shelton Hensley, the author's great-great grandparents

Hensley William

Co. B, 16 North Carolina Inf.
(Formerly 6 N. C. Infantry. Vols.)
(Confederate,)

Fifer   Private

CARD NUMBERS.

1 485 46 410	20
2 6536	21
3 6590	22
4	23
5	24
6	25
7	26
8	27
9	28
10	29
11	30
12	31
13	32
14	33
15	34
16	35
17	36
18	37
19	38

Number of medical cards herein ___2___

Number of personal papers herein ___2___

BOOK MARK: ___________________

See also ___________________

Wm Hensley
Co. B. 16th N. C.

Appears on a

Receipt Roll

for clothing of Lieutenant, subsequently Captain, W. Kemp Tabb's Company, Camp Guard at Camp Winder, Richmond, Va.

Roll dated ______________________

__________ Not dated _______, 186 .

Date of issue _March 25_, 1863 .

Signature _Wm Hensley_

Remarks: _____________________

Book mark: _____________________

(653)   Copyist.
8144

H | 16 | N.C.

William Hensly

Pvt., Co. B, { 16 Reg't North Carolina Infantry (State Troops).

Appears on

Company Muster Roll

of the organization named above,

for _July & Aug_, 1863.

Enlisted:
When _Apr. 29_, 1861.
Where _Marshall N.C._
By whom _Capt Peek_
Period _1 yr._
Last paid:
By whom _Capt Hill_
To what time _June 30_, 1863.

Present or absent _Present_

Remarks:

This regiment was organized in May, 1861, with twelve companies, A to M. Companies A and L were transferred by S. O. No. 116, A. & I. G. O., dated May 20, 1862, and became (1st) Company A and Company E, respectively, Infantry Regiment, Thomas' Legion North Carolina Troops.

The designation of this regiment was changed from the 6th Regiment North Carolina Infantry (Volunteers) to the 16th Regiment North Carolina Infantry (State Troops) by S. O. No. 222, A. & I. G. O., dated November 14, 1861.

Book mark:

E. O. Leech
Copyist.

(442)

H | 16 | N.C.

W. Hansley

Co. B, 16 Reg't, N.C.

Appears on a Register of

**Receiving and Wayside Hospital,
or General Hospital No. 9,
Richmond, Virginia.**

Date _Feb 25_, 1865.
Transferred to _Gen. Elzey's Office_

Remarks:

Confed. Arch., Chap. 6, File No. 114, page 682.

J. C. Johnson
Sergt.
Copyist.

(535)

| H | 16 | N.C. |

Wm. Hensley
Pvt., Co. B, { 16 Reg't North Carolina
Infantry (State Troops).

Appears on

Company Muster Roll

of the organization named above,

for _Jan. & Feb._ 186_3_.

Enlisted:
When _Apr. 29_ , 186_1_.
Where _Marshall N.C._
By whom _Capt Peek_
Period _War_
Last paid:
By whom _Capt Summerey_
To what time _Dec. 31_ , 186_2_.

Present or absent _Absent_
Remarks: _Detailed to Hospital_
Richmond Va Feb 28, 1863

This regiment was organized in May, 1861, with twelve
companies, A to M. Companies A and L were transferred by
S. O. No. 114, A. & I. G. O., dated May 20, 1862, and became
(1st) Company A and Company E, respectively, Infantry
Regiment, Thomas' Legion North Carolina Troops.

The designation of this regiment was changed from the 6th
Regiment North Carolina Infantry (Volunteers) to the 16th
Regiment North Carolina Infantry (State Troops) by S. O. No.
232, A. & I. G. O., dated November 14, 1861.

Book mark :

(642) _E. O. Peek_
Copyist.

| H | 16 | N.C |

William Hensley
Fifer, Co. B, { 6 Reg't North Carolina
Infantry (Volunteers).

Appears on

Company Muster Roll

of the organization named above,

for _Apr. 29 ' to Aug. 31_, 186_1_

Enlisted:
When _Apr. 29_ , 186
Where _Marshall_
By whom _Capt Peek_
Period _12 mos_
Last paid:
By whom
To what time , 186

Present or absent _Present_
Remarks:

This regiment was organized in May, 1861, with twelve
companies, A to M. Companies A and L were transferred by
S. O. No. 114, A. & I. G. O., dated May 20, 1862, and became
(1st) Company A and Company E, respectively, Infantry
Regiment, Thomas' Legion North Carolina Troops.

The designation of this regiment was changed from the 6th
Regiment North Carolina Infantry (Volunteers) to the 16th
Regiment North Carolina Infantry (State Troops) by S. O. No.
232, A. & I. G. O., dated November 14, 1861.

Book mark :

(642) _E. O. Peek_
Copyist.

THE CONFEDERATE STATES, Dr.

To _W^m Hensly_

_Co B 16. N.C. 2d_   **C. S. Army.**

	DOLLARS	CTS.
For Monthly Pay, from _June 20th_ 186_3_ to _Aug 31st_ 186_3_		
being _3_ months, _ _ days, at _$11_ per month,	33	00
For Clothing from Apl 24th 1861 to Oct 8th 1861		
being 5 mos & 15 days at $4.15 pr mo	23	16
For Clothing from Oct 8th 1861 to Aug 31st 1863		
being 10 mos & 23 days at 11.16 pr mo	120	09
For Subsistence from Richmond Va to Morehead		
Deduct, due _N.C. being 586 miles at one ration per day &c &c_	15	99
for Clothing Drawn	22	25
Amount paid,	$151	65

I certify, that I have endorsed this Payment on _Hensly_ Descriptive Roll.

Discharge

RECEIVED, _Richmond_ this _2_ day of _Sept_ 186_3_

from _Maj John Ambler_ Quartermaster C. S. Army, the sum of

One Hundred fifty one 65/100 Dollars,

being the amount, and in full of the above account.

WITNESS,

Wm Hensly

____

[Signed Duplicates.]

Richmond,   186

Personally appeared before me, a

_ _ Co. (_duplicate_).   Regt.   Vols., and made oath

that he is without a descriptive roll or final statement, which it is impossible to obtain from his com-

manding officer, for the reason that his company is now

that the above account, amounting to _ _ 100 Dollars,

is correct; that he is not in debt to the Confederate States, and that he will present a statement of this

payment to his commanding officer.

J. S. Dunawall

Capt & AQM

Chapter Eight
Matilda and Nancy: The Shelton Sisters Who Became Hensley Wives

The ways of the author's kinship to Matilda Shelton:

1. Me---Edd Shelton---Joe Shelton---Avarinza Hensley---Matilda Shelton
2. Me---Velma King---Woolsey King---Matilda Haire---Nick Haire---Matilda Shelton

Matilda Shelton is my great-great grandmother one way and my great-great-great grandmother another way.

The ways of the author's kinship to Nancy Shelton:

1. Me---Edd Shelton---Nellie Hensley---Bevy Hensley---Nancy Shelton
2. Me---Velma King---Woolsey King---George King (Hensley)---Nancy Shelton

Nancy Shelton is my great-great grandmother two different ways.

Matilda Shelton was born December 23, 1831, the oldest daughter of Bill and Cloey Riddle Shelton. She married Robert Nelson Hawkins F. Haire in 1848, and they had the following children; Laura (1849), Millard (1850) (killed in the ambush on Butt Mountain July 19, 1864), Nicholas Wooten (1853), Julia (1856), William (1859), and Martha (1862). Robert Haire's parents were Abraham Haire and Sarah Rebecca Waddell. Sarah's parents were John Waddell and Rebecca Sevier, daughter of John Sevier (first governor of Tennessee) and Sarah Hawkins. When Abraham Haire married Sarah Rebecca Waddell, the Sevier family disapproved of the marriage and disowned her, so Abraham and Sarah moved from Tennessee to Shelton Laurel, North Carolina to settle down and raise their family.

I feel the need to interject some information concerning John Sevier, the first governor of Tennessee. A lot of people claim kinship to this colorful historical figure, and the fact that he fathered eighteen children, makes most of their claims legitimate! Here is my kinship. John Sevier and Sarah Hawkins---Rebecca Sevier and John Waddell, Jr.---Sarah Rebecca Waddell and Abraham Haire---Robert Haire and MATILDA SHELTON---Nicholas Wooten (Nick) Haire and Tolitha Hall---Matilda Haire and George King---Woolsey King and Doshia Cutshaw---Velma King and Edd Shelton---ME.

John Sevier was from Virginia, and in the 1770s moved his wife Sarah and their family to the area of Tennessee that is present-day Elizabethton. At some point he was given the nickname of Nolichucky Jack. John Sevier gained the reputation of being an outstanding Indian fighter, frontiersman, and politician. After the Revolutionary War began, he and other frontiersmen built Fort Caswell, also known as Fort Watauga, on the banks of the Watauga River. The present-day Sycamore Shoals State Park depicts Fort Watauga. In July of 1776, the fort was occupied by several hundred women and children and was guarded by less than one hundred well-armed men. On July 21, 1776, some of the women had went outside the fort to milk cows when suddenly hundreds of Cherokees began to attack.

The men sounded the alarm and closed and barred the entrance to the fort. One twenty-two year old woman was locked outside the fort. With bullets and arrows flying everywhere, she ran like a deer to one of the side walls of the fort and jumped as high as she could, grabbing hold of the top of the wall. She climbed over the wall with the help of a hand that appeared and fell into the arms of John Sevier. This young woman's name was Catherine Sherrill, affectionately known as "Bonnie Kate". John Sevier was currently married to Sarah Hawkins, but evidently something happened at that meeting at the wall of the fort, because when Sarah died shortly after giving birth to their tenth child, Rebecca in 1780, four months later John Sevier and Bonnie Kate were married. She later bare him eight more children.

John Sevier took a leadership role in the Battle of King's Mountain in 1780, and later in the same year led a group of frontiersmen in defeating the Cherokees at Boyd's Creek in present-day Sevier County, Tennessee. After the

Revolutionary War, politician John Sevier led a movement to form a new state from the western lands of North Carolina. He was elected governor of the state of Franklin in 1785, but the state was never recognized by the government, and by 1788, John Sevier was arrested and convicted of treason, but was later pardoned after he pledged allegiance to the state of North Carolina. For the next few years he represented North Carolina in the House of Representatives. When the state of Tennessee was formed in 1796, John Sevier was elected governor and moved to Knoxville. He served as governor of Tennessee from 1796 to 1801 and again from 1803 to 1809. John Sevier had his enemies, one being Andrew Jackson. After Sevier publicly accused Jackson of adultery, Jackson challenged him to a duel, upon which Sevier readily accepted. The duel never occurred due to various circumstances, however. John Sevier died in 1815, and is buried in Knoxville. To readers of this manuscript not from Tennessee this information may help explain why there are many streets, schools, communities, and even a county in east Tennessee named in honor of John Sevier, my sixth great grandfather.

Now back to the story of Matilda. When the Civil War began, Robert Haire became a Union Partisan Fighter. Robert was killed on September 17, 1863, by a band of Rebel soldiers from the 64th regiment that was in the Laurel region at the time conscripting and pillaging. His death left Matilda a young widow with six children to raise. She married John Hensley shortly after the war and they had three children of their own; Avarinza (May 30, 1867), (This is why the author's family reunion and cemetery decoration is always Memorial Day weekend. It began as a celebration of Avarinza's birthday.), George (1869), and Emily (1876). John Hensley was a son of Charles and Rhoda Franklin Hensley. Matilda Shelton died February 2, 1894, and is buried in the Judith Shelton cemetery alongside of her first in-laws, Abraham and Sarah Rebecca Waddell Haire. John Hensley, her second husband, died March 18, 1900, and was buried alongside an infant on a hill overlooking B. E. and Avarinza Hensley Shelton's farm.

In 1912, when Dube Shelton died as a young man, B. E. and Avarinza decided to bury their son on an adjacent hill, and as the years passed and other family members died, they were buried alongside Dube. In 1980, descendants of B. E. and Avarinza got the necessary approval and paperwork to move the remains of John Hensley and the infant to the different location. The author participated in the move, and it was apparent when we exhumed John's remains why the decision was made to change the location of the cemetery. The lower two feet of John's grave was hewn out of solid rock. The grave was still six feet deep, but the family evidently decided then and there that they weren't going to dig any other graves into a bed of rock!

Today, the B. E. Shelton Cemetery is maintained by the family, and it is one of the most beautiful cemeteries in Madison County. This cemetery is also referred to as the Elbridge Shelton Cemetery (B. E. stands for Bluford Elbridge).The annual decoration and memorial service is the Sunday before Memorial Day, and in 2013, we celebrated the 100th anniversary of that occasion.

Nancy Shelton was born February 14, 1837, so she was a little over five years younger than Matilda. There had been two boys born between the two sisters, Noah and William Riley. These two sisters had younger sisters Minerva Jane, Isabel Dansel, and Iona that was mentioned in the July 24, 1863 edition of the *New York Times*. This was the same article that recounted the story of the Shelton Laurel Massacre. Quoting the article: *"The daughters of William Shelton, a man of wealth and highly respectable, were demanded by some of the officers to play and sing for them. They played and sang a few national songs. Keith learned of it, and ordered that the ladies be placed under arrest, and sent to the guard-house, where they remained all night. And the men who did this were called soldiers."* I take it that these girls refused to sing *"Dixie"* for the Rebel officers. This is the first indication that I have found as to the origin of musical talent that is so prevalent in the Shelton family.

Nancy Shelton married George W. Franklin, Jr. and they had one son, Barnett Shelton. For some reason he didn't take the Franklin name. Shortly after he was born, Nancy and George Franklin divorced. She married Ellison King and George married Drury Norton's widow, Nancy Shelton Norton. Nancy and Ellison had the following children; America (1857), William Ervin (1860), and Sarah (1863). Nancy was evidently pregnant with Sarah when Ellison was captured and executed in the Shelton Laurel Massacre. After Bill Hensley (John Hensley's brother) returned home from his duty with the 16th Confederate regiment, he and Nancy began living together and they had the following children; George (1865), Thomas Jefferson (1868), Burgess (1869), Bevy (1872), Ben (1876) and Mattie (1878). As was stated in the chapter on Bill Hensley, after finally being able to marry, Nancy and Bill lived a long full life and are buried side by side in the Union Chapel Cemetery in Greene County, Tennessee (Nancy died on March 20, 1920). I asked my grandfather Woolsey King if he remembered his grandmother Nancy, and all that he could tell me was that everybody called her "grandma Nan." I would have loved to have been able to sit down with my two great-great grandmothers Matilda and Nancy and had a long conversation with them about the war and how it affected their lives, but I know that isn't possible. In the after-life when I see them, we won't be talking about anything adverse or bad, only the good and Godly things will be discussed.

Matilda Shelton Haire Hensley, the author's great-great grandmother

Burial site of Matilda Shelton Haire Hensley

Burial site of Abraham and Sara Rebecca Waddell Haire, the parents of Matilda's first husband, Robert

Burial site of John Hensley, Matilda's second husband and the author's great-great grandfather

Burial site of Nick and Tolitha Hall Riddle Haire, the author's great-great grandparents

Chapter Nine
The Three "T's": Trees, Tobacco, Tomatoes

One can only imagine what Roderick Shelton, his wife Sarah, and their sons Martin and David saw when they entered the valley that is now called Shelton Laurel, North Carolina in the 1780s. The forests had never been timbered or cut, the old growth hardwoods of American chestnut, yellow poplar, oaks, and maples predominated the coves, while pines and other gymnosperms dominated the ridges. Huge hemlock trees grew close to the creek banks, while understory species of mountain laurel, rhododendrons, dogwoods and redbuds grew under the canopy of the climax forest. Today, not one square foot of the virgin forests remain in Shelton Laurel, so we can't fathom the size and girth of the trees that the original settlers saw. There are currently very few pockets of virgin forests left in the southern Appalachians. One 3,800 acre stand is located near Robbinsville, North Carolina, called the Joyce Kilmer Memorial Forest. A visitor can see poplar and hemlock trees approaching ten feet in diameter. Joyce Kilmer was a very devout Roman Catholic poet from New Jersey who was killed in action in the Second Battle of the Marne (1918 in France), during World War I. His most famous poem is simply entitled *"Trees."* It is worth quoting at this time:

Trees

"I think that I shall never see
A poem as lovely as a tree.
A tree whose hungry mouth is pressed
Against the earth's sweet flowing breast.
A tree that looks at God all day
And lifts her leafy arms to pray.
A tree that may in summer wear
A nest of robins in her hair.
Upon whose bosom snow has lain
Who intimately lives with rain
Poems are made by fools like me
But only God can make a tree."

This is a simple poem with an astronomical meaning. Old growth trees were several hundred years old. Now when we see a tree that is five feet in diameter we think it is a huge tree. As was stated earlier, old growth poplar and hemlock trees can be up to ten feet through! When Martin Shelton decided to settle in what is now called the Little Laurel section of present-day Madison County, family tradition states that he lived in a hollow poplar tree for several months until he got his cabin built. One cold evening he was keeping warm by partaking of some homemade "refreshment" and, in his somewhat inebriated condition, fell asleep with his feet at the entrance to his "tree" house, and woke up with frostbitten toes. Realizing that the frostbite would lead to gangrene and eventually death, he amputated his own toes, and lived to marry and have a large family. It is not known if he became a teetotaler after that incident.

The only trees that were cut before the War Between the States were the ones needed for building cabins, barns, fences, and wood used for heating and cooking. Trees from the leveler areas of the forests were cut to clear land for the settlers' meager crops. Trees in narrow coves, steeper hills, and ridges were left alone. All along Shelton Laurel Creek there is an average of a one-fourth mile wide flood plain. This land was cleared first, and this is where most of the original farms were located. After the war, times were hard for the families who had lost loved ones. Some of the widows were eligible for financial compensation, while others were not. When reconstruction began nationwide shortly after the war, lumber became a much needed commodity. Eventually, the virgin forests of Shelton Laurel and all of the mountains of Madison County were viewed upon as "green gold" by northern timber and lumber companies. For several decades after the war, any able-bodied man (or older boy) willing to work could get a job and earn an income by working in the timber harvesting industry in the Shelton Laurel region.

The first timber harvesting company to begin operations in the area was the Scottish Carolina Timber and Land Company, with head offices in Glasgow, Scotland. The general manager of the American entity was Alexander

A. Arthur. He had discovered a huge stand of virgin timber in the Pigeon River watershed that he had proposed using the river itself to transport the cut timber to Newport, Tennessee. A series of booms were constructed along the river and also the French Broad River downstream of where the Pigeon enters the larger river. Hundreds of local men and foreigners from mainly Canada proceeded to clear-cut the forests using steam-powered timber harvesting equipment and the river to float the logs downstream to Newport. All of this occurred from the early 1880s to the spring of 1886. Then disaster struck. It had already been a very wet spring, and the rivers were running very full. Then a series of cloudbursts hit the upper Pigeon watershed, and the already swollen waters of the Pigeon River and French Broad River rose dramatically. Dammed up behind the booms were thousands of logs, but the raging river washed out the booms, and the fortune in logs were washed away. This disaster spelled the end of Mr. Arthur's timber harvesting venture. After the water receded, logs were found in the Tennessee and Mississippi Rivers and even the Gulf of Mexico. The precedent had been established, however, and soon other timber companies began operations in the mountains.

In the meantime, the railroad had been completed in January of 1882, from Asheville to Paint Rock, connecting the people of Madison County to the outside world. The railroad followed the same course as the Buncombe Turnpike and therefore brought an end to the era of the hog and turkey drives and put out of business all of the stock stands and taverns along the turnpike.

From that point on, timber companies didn't have to rely on the French Broad River to transport their logs. They could now utilize rail transportation to ship their product. One of the first and largest timber harvesting companies to begin operations in Madison County was the Betts Lumber Company with headquarters in New York. This company bought timber-harvesting rights in the virgin forests of Shelton Laurel, Little Laurel, and Big Laurel regions all the way to the Tennessee state line. They built a large mill for sawing the timber into lumber where the Laurel River flows into the French Broad River at Runion. From there, they laid railroad spurs up Little Laurel and Shelton Laurel all the way to the Flint Mountain at the head of upper Mill Creek. Old rotting, moss-covered trestles are still standing crossing ravines in the Deep Cut and Big Cove regions of Mill Creek not far from the Appalachian Trail. (The author owns an eighteen inch long piece of rail from the Mill Creek spur that is used as an anvil.)

It was at this time that anybody in Shelton Laurel that wanted a job could get a job in the timber industry. In 1914, The Curry brothers from Andrews, North Carolina came to Shelton Laurel and bought timber-harvesting rights of the Hickey's Fork watershed from the Betts Lumber Company. They built a large band mill where Hickey's Fork Creek empties into Shelton Laurel Creek, and several logging camps in the area became established. This occurred shortly after a second devastating flood hit Madison County in 1916, eventually causing the Betts Lumber Company to go bankrupt. The Curry brothers' logging camps grew rapidly into a township with several hundred residents, all working in timber and lumber jobs. The town was given a name, Druid, and even had a post office. The author's great-grandfather's, brother, Bayliss Shelton, was instrumental in getting a primitive telephone line up Shelton Laurel at that time, but without adequate funding and maintenance, it was very short-lived. After around eight years of aggressive timber harvesting and clear-cutting, the virgin forests of Shelton Laurel were gone. Left instead were erosion-inducing logging roads, streams and creeks full of siltation (which led to the virtual extinction of the native Brook Trout), soil that was so damaged that it wasn't hardly fit for crops, and lots of Shelton Laurel residents out of work. So the people of Shelton Laurel had to come up with another way to put food on their table. Enter the tobacco-growing era.

The first person to grow tobacco commercially in America was John Rolf in 1612, in Virginia, to be exported to England. In 1619, the Inspection Act regulated the sale of tobacco, and the government has had its hand in regulating farm commodities ever since. North Carolina was the second state to produce tobacco, with Kentucky and Tennessee following soon after. Growing tobacco is very labor intensive, and since the mountain farmers of western North Carolina were too poor to own slaves, not much tobacco was grown in the years preceding the Civil War, and the war itself greatly diminished the male work force. After the timber industry in essence ran out of trees to harvest, farmers of Shelton Laurel started growing more tobacco. The flue-cured tobacco varieties that was grown in large amounts in the Piedmont and coastal parts of the state did not grow well in the mountains, so farmers started growing burley tobacco. Burley is air-cured and the climate of the mountains is better suited for the air-curing process.

By the 1880s, there were several thousand tobacco factories across the country producing snuff, cigars, pipe and chewing tobacco, and eventually cigarettes. By the 1930s increased production led to great pricing swings, and the farmers of the mountains often didn't make any profit at all. The Agricultural Adjustment Act of 1938 placed marketing quotas on the amount of tobacco each farm could produce. However, the good thing that came from that act was that farmers were guaranteed a fair price for their tobacco even if companies chose not to bid on their crop at the auction warehouse. For about the first thirty years of the quota system, farmers were assigned an acreage allotment. A government representative would come to the farm in the spring and measure the field or fields where the farmer indicated that tobacco would be grown. Dishonest farmers could very easily grow more tobacco than their acreage allotment allowed by having fields not measured by the government representative. In the 1960s, the acreage allotment was changed for a poundage allotment, which was a much fairer system.

In 1954, domestic tobacco production reached its peak, with North Carolina and Kentucky leading the way. Madison County was consistently the number one burley tobacco-producing county in North Carolina. Before my grandfather Woolsey King got his first truck, he would take a horse-drawn wagon full of packed tobacco to market at the warehouses of either Asheville, North Carolina, Johnson City or Greeneville, Tennessee. He would be gone sometimes as long as a week at a time. An interesting observation of the author is that I never saw my grandfather actually "working" in the tobacco fields. He would always hire help or have some tenants living in houses that he owned to do the manual labor. I did, however, observe my grandmother Doshia in the tobacco barn pulling the leaves off the stalks and grading them often in the fall of the year. I guess my grandfather Woolsey figured out early on how to be the "boss" and not the "worker".

By the 1960s, reports started being published that warned of the many health risks and hazards associated with tobacco use, and domestic demand and production of tobacco began to slowly decline. There are still farms in Shelton Laurel that produce burley tobacco, even though the allotment, quota system and price support guaranteed by the government ended in 2004. Small acreage farms generally don't grow tobacco, and the larger farms can grow as much as they want, with no guarantee of any profit. Owners of large farms usually pay migrant workers to do the intense labor. It is estimated that by the year 2050 virtually no tobacco will be produced or used in the United States, and it is this author's opinion that "that is a good thing".

One of the many chores that the mountaineer wife had to learn and perform was the proper canning of fruits and vegetables. As was alluded to in a previous chapter, refrigerators and freezers weren't an option when it came to preserving food for later use. Electricity didn't make it to Shelton Laurel until the 1940s. The author's family home place in upper Mill Creek got electricity in 1948. Proper canning is an art and a craft that is quickly disappearing now simply because of the lack of necessity.

The Stokely family in Newport, Tennessee was so proficient in canning methods that they decided to open a small cannery after the death of the father. The widow Stokely had nine children, and all of them became involved in the growing and canning of vegetables. By the 1930s, their little canning enterprise had grown into a multi-million dollar business.

The farmers of Shelton Laurel began to diversify and grow more than just tobacco. The author's grandfather Joe Shelton started growing green beans to sell to the Stokely cannery in Newport. Also, farmers started producing tomatoes. As the years passed after World War II, a lot of tomatoes were grown. At some point in the 1960s, the production of tomatoes even eclipsed the production of tobacco. Boxes upon boxes of tomatoes were harvested just as they began the ripening process and trucked to Newport, the closest tomato grading facility. After they were graded they were sold to the cannery in Newport. The author's grandfather, Woolsey King, was one of the largest tomato producers in Shelton Laurel.

I remember him coming to our farm in Greene County, Tennessee, every summer to collect all of the twine that we had cut off our hay bales the preceding winter in feeding our cattle. He would then use the twine to tie up the tomato vines in his fields to keep the developing tomatoes from touching the ground, as that would promote rotting, and decrease the harvest yield. In 1969 Woolsey along with some other farmers of Shelton Laurel built a tomato-grading facility on Shelton Laurel Creek just downstream from the then newly built sanctuary of the Carmen Church of God. This greatly expedited the tomato-production process.

There are still farms in Shelton Laurel that grow tomatoes today, even though the tomato "shed" is no longer in use. The Stokely cannery expanded and eventually bought out Van Camp in Indiana, and later merged with Bush Brothers. The timber industry is making a modest comeback, as it's been 80 to 100 years since clear-cutting devastated the forests. It takes trees between 70 to 100 years to become mature enough to be harvested, so timber that is being cut today are second generation trees and not virgin forests. My father Edd Shelton's first job was working at his future father-in-law Woolsey King's sawmill for 12.5 cents per hour. Later he trucked pulp wood to Runion (he called it "Stackhouse") before he and my mother Velma were married.

The one species of tree that isn't making a comeback is the American chestnut (*Castanea dentata*). These trees grew to over one hundred feet tall and was at one time the dominant hardwood tree in the climax forests of Southern Appalachia. Around 1904, some Chinese chestnut tree seedlings were imported that were infected with the fungus *Cryphonectria parasitica*. The Chinese varieties of chestnut trees were resistant to this fungus, but the American species of chestnut was very vulnerable to the parasitic fungus, and by the 1950s, had virtually disappeared from the forests. However, with selective cross-fertilization and genetic engineering, botany departments of several universities have produced seeds that are almost 100% pure American chestnuts. The genetically engineered DNA contains fungus-resistant genes, so hopefully we can once again see the eastern forests of North America bountiful with these magnificent trees.

Since the early 1900s, the three "T's", trees, tobacco, and tomatoes, have made the people of Shelton Laurel a lot of money. Today, with the improved road system in Madison and surrounding counties, most work-force aged people in Shelton Laurel travel to public employment in Asheville, Greeneville, Erwin, or Johnson City. There are, however, a few inhabitants that still make their living off the land. Hurrah to them!

William Riley Shelton, the author's great-great grandfather

Burial site of William Riley Shelton

B.E. and Avarinza Hensley Shelton, the author's great-grandparents

Bevy and Sylvinnia Ray Hensley, the author's great-grandparents

Joe and Nellie Hensley Shelton, the author's paternal grandparents

Woolsey and Doshia Cutshaw King, the author's maternal grandparents

Chapter Ten

The Farmer Goes to War:
The Story of Edd Shelton's Military Service

Dad and Mom (Edd and Velma) were married on November 27, 1941. Just ten days later, the Japanese bombed Pearl Harbor, and the U. S. declared war on Japan. Just after that, Germany declared war on the U. S. Dad was drafted twice during the next two years, but was deferred because they were farmers, and farming was their only source of income. However, as the war dragged on and the military needed more soldiers, Dad was finally drafted in June 1944, and was mustered in on June 26, 1944, at Fort Bragg, North Carolina. He did his basic training at Camp Blanding, Florida. After finishing basic training, he was sent back to Camp Blanding to train for the war in the Pacific, as the war in Europe was apparently going to be over soon. (After June 6, 1944, the Allies were pushing quickly towards Germany.) Mother even moved to Florida for a little while and lived just off the base in Gainesville.

In December 1944, the Germans mounted a massive counterattack and moved the front far to the west. This was known as the Ardennes Offensive, or the Battle of the Bulge. Dad was quickly sent to France, and on

January 1, 1945, joined up with Company H, 347th Regiment of the 87th Infantry Division (the Golden Acorn Division) and sent to the front lines as a machine gunner. This was a part of the 3rd Army, commanded by Gen. George Patton.

Dad went through Bastogne, Belgium, just a few days after the 101st Airborne division was rescued from siege there. He said the town was nothing but rubble due to all of the bombing. Early in January, his company had to travel through waist-deep snow, but by mid-January a warm front came in and then they had to travel through knee-deep mud. The 347th's assignment was to go into a town that had been heavily bombed and clean out any German resistance. Dad said they would camp on the outskirts of the town at night, because after dark the Germans would bomb the town, thinking the allies were in town. This town-hopping continued east, Dad went through Luxemburg, and by late January was real close to the Germany border on the Sauer River.

The worst battle by far that Dad was engaged in occurred the day and night of February 2, 1945, in a little town in Belgium. Dad saw a 2nd Lieutenant get shot between the eyes, as he peeked around the side of a building. Later, in the day, a sergeant was mortally wounded, and while dying, was screaming loudly. Dad said the medic stuffed his mouth full of snow so he would die quietly and not divulge their position. Later in the evening, Dad was lying in a pile of dirty snow and mud and he heard a mortar come in and hit right beside him. He reached behind him and felt the hole in the mud where it was submerged, but it was a "dud" and didn't explode. A little later one did explode close to him and he was wounded by shrapnel in his thigh, but that wound didn't take him out of action. By the next morning, Dad's platoon was virtually wiped out, but the Germans had run out of ammunition during the night, so Dad and five other soldiers took captive over 100 German prisoners. Dad was offered a field promotion to sergeant but turned it down. He did, however, agree to be the temporary squad leader, and drew sergeant's pay for the next ten days.

Dad said that one evening he was in a foxhole and a jeep pulled up. The soldier on guard duty yelled *"Halt, who goes there?"* The voice from the jeep answered, *"Well, they call me Ike around here."* This "Ike" went on to become President of the United States from 1952 to 1960. Also, Dad said they would drop cigarettes and candy bars from airplanes to the troops. Dad didn't smoke, so he would trade his Lucky Strikes for Hershey bars, melt them using his helmet for a pot, and drink the hot chocolate. Dad saw Gen. Patton (wearing his ivory-handled pistol) several times.

On February 12, 1945, he was at the Belgium-German border in sight of the Siegfried line, when a sniper's bullet hit him in the ankle. At that time the combat ended for Dad. He rode all the next day in an ambulance back across France and then was transported to a hospital in Liverpool, England, where he spent the next four months. While he was there the Germans surrendered after Hitler's suicide, and the war in Europe ended.

In July of 1945, Dad was sent to a rehab facility run by the Army right on the beach in Daytona, Florida. Dad would come home to Shelton Laurel virtually every weekend by train, and on October 26, 1945, was honorably discharged and came home for good.

Dad earned two Purple Hearts and was awarded several medals, including the Bronze Star. He never would talk about his war experience to us , and only during his last few months at home before having to move to a nursing home did he open up to me with specific information about the war.

Edd and Velma King Shelton, the author's parents

Maynard Scott Shelton, was born at 7:20 A.M., Sunday, January 22, 1956, at Takoma Hospital and Sanitarium in Greeneville, Tennessee. I am the fourth and last child of Edd and Velma King Shelton. My parents owned a small farm in the Carmen community of Shelton Laurel, North Carolina until 1950. At that time they sold that farm and bought forty-two acres in the Rheatown community of Greene County, Tennessee. My father had been wounded while serving in the army during World War II, and was having trouble farming with horse-drawn implements on hillsides. Shortly after purchasing the Rheatown, TN. property, he traded a nearly new pickup truck for a used Farmall Super-A tractor and some implements. So I was born into a farming family. We had "milch" cows and a tobacco allotment for income, and raised corn and hay for the feeding of the livestock. I never moved off the farm, and in 1992, I purchased the farm and house that they had built in 1959, with the understanding that it would remain theirs for their use until their death. Edd died in 2000 and Velma died in 2013, and they are buried in the B. E. Shelton Cemetery at the head of Mill Creek in Shelton Laurel, North Carolina.

I was educated at Chuckey Elementary School and Chuckey-Doak High School, where I graduated ranked third in class ranking in 1974. I played varsity baseball for three years and was named to the all-district team my senior year. My hobbies were searching the farm for arrowheads (it still is; over the years I've found around 400 artifacts), studying the games of baseball and football, and hiking. I never did really get into hunting and fishing, although I used to do some of both. Over the years I've become somewhat of an environmentalist, and have decided that the best place to hunt meat to eat is in the meat department of the supermarket. Another hobby that I really enjoy is farming. I count it as a hobby and not a livelihood, as there's no way that I could make a living and pay all of the bills on the farm income like my parents did. Also, while very young, I developed and have maintained a keen interest in traditional music being performed on acoustic stringed instruments. The Joe and Nellie Hensley Shelton descendants have a family reunion on Memorial Day weekend on the grounds of the old home place on upper Mill Creek, and some of my early memories involve listening to and watching my uncles play and sing bluegrass music, so naturally I developed my musical talent along that genre of music.

I was awarded an Alumni Scholarship and matching Foundation Grant to attend East Tennessee State University (ETSU) in Johnson City, Tennessee. I graduated as *Magna Cum Laude*, with a grade point average of 3.79 with a major in Microbiology and an emphasis in Pre-medicine Studies, in 1978. After being denied admission to medical school, I continued my post-graduate studies at ETSU after being awarded a Graduate Teaching Assistantship. It was at this point that I received my first professional experience in teaching. I graduated with a Master's Degree in Microbiology and Biochemistry (GPA of 4.00) in 1982. I was immediately hired by Bristol College in Bristol, Tennessee, and was an Assistant Professor and later an Associate Professor in the Medical Assistant program there. In 1986, I began taking education courses at ETSU so that I could become certified as a science teacher in secondary schools in Tennessee. In January of 1987, I resigned my professorship at Bristol College to student- teach for a semester at Sullivan South High School in Sullivan County, Tennessee. Upon completion of course work, I became certified to teach any science course offered in any secondary curriculum in Tennessee. In September of 1987, I was hired to be the Biology teacher at South Greene High School in Greene County, Tennessee. In 1989, I switched over to become the Chemistry, Physics, and Ecology teacher for SGHS. At the time of this writing, I am teaching my 28th year at South Greene High School.

This manuscript is the result of me being continually dismayed or disappointed by reading articles and even books written by non-family members about the Sheltons and other families and the hardships they had to endure while living in Shelton Laurel, North Carolina. Non-family authors tend to be careless with the facts. Historians working on a dissertation cannot feel the empathy I feel because it's not their great-great-great grandparents they're writing about. Actually, writing this manuscript is one of the items on my "bucket list." One more unfulfilled dream remains. When I get a cabin built on my Mill Creek property, I guess I'll be ready for the Lord to call me to my *"... LONG HOME..."*!!! (*Ecclesiastes. 12:5, KJV*)

Publications by the Author

"Response of *Salmonella typhimurium* Mutants to Delta-9 Tetrahydrocannabinol and in Conjunction with Known Mutagens", published in:

1. *Journal Of Environmental Science and Health,* A18(3), Pgs. 413-443(1983)
2. *The Cannabinoids: Chemical, Pharmacologic, and Therapeutic Aspects,* Pgs. 751-774. Academic Press, Inc. (Harcourt Brace Jovanovich) (1984)

"Water Quality Parameters of Camp Creek" *TVA Water Quality Monitoring Network Yearbook,* Vol. 1, !990

"Matilda Shelton Haire Hensley", *Madison County Heritage, North Carolina, Vol. II,* Pg. 134

"William (Bill) Hensley", *Madison County Heritage, North Carolina, Vol. II,* Pg. 134

Discography of the Author

Christmas Guitar, A collection of instrumental sacred Christmas songs (1996)

Finger-picking Classics, A collection of the author's favorite songs performed on guitar with no plectrum (2010)

Bibliography of Sources

Arthur, John Preston, *Western North Carolina: A History (1730-1913)*. Ch. XXVII. Raleigh, North Carolina, Edwards and Broughton Printing Company,1914.

Crow, Vernon H. *Storm in the Mountains: Thomas' Legion of Cherokee Indians and Mountaineers*, Cherokee, North Carolina, Press of the Cherokee Indian, 1982.

Dykeman, Wilma, *The French Broad*, New York, New York, Rinehart and Company, Inc., 1955.

Ellis, Daniel, *Thrilling Adventures of Daniel Ellis*, New York, New York, Harper and Brothers, Publishers, 1867 (Repinted, 1971)

Fletcher, Earl W. Jr., *Off The Laurel: The Place and the People*, Earl Fletcher, Jr., Publisher, 2001.

Hensley, Clay, and Zelois Shelton Hensley, *The Sheltons*, Huntsville, Alabama, Clay Hensley, Publisher, 1985.

Hensley, Zelois Shelton, Family Historian, "Oral Histories", (aunt of the author).

LeMasters, Larry, *Civil War Times, Illustrated*, "Die Like a Damned Dog", Premedia Enthusiast Publications, Inc., Vol. XXXVIII, No. 4, August, 1999.

Madison County Heritage, North Carolina, Vol. I, 1994. And *Madison County Heritage, North Carolina, Vol. II*, 2000.

National Archives and Records Admimistration, "Military Records", Washington, D. C., 20408.

Paludan, Phillip Shaw, *Victims: A True Story of the Civil War*, Knoxville, Tennessee, The University of Tennessee Press, 1981.

Ready, Milton, *Mystical Madison: The History of a Mountain Region*, Lynn, North Carolina., EverReady Publications, 2011.

Shelton, William "Bud", *The Sheltons and Shelton Laurel*, unpublished manuscript, 1963. (copy in author's possession)

Shelton, Z. F. *The Sheltons*, Montgomery, Alabama, Z. F. Shelton, Publisher, 1962.

The Madison News Record Sentinel, Marshall, North Carolina newspaper

The New York Times, July 24, 1863.

Tobacco Profile-Agricultural Marketing Resource Center

Trotter, William R., *Bushwhackers: The Civil War in North Carolina; The Mountains*, Winston Salem, North Carolina, John F. Blair, Publisher, 1982.

Wellman, Manley Wade, *Kingdom of Madison*, Chapel Hill: University of North Carolina Press, 1971.

Whitaker, Mildred Campbell, *The Sheltons of England and America*, St. Louis, Missouri, The Mound Press, 1941

Wikipedia, Internet Encyclopedia